A Pocketful of Stars

William and Noelene Morris

Dedicated to
The Great Solution

First published in 1994 by
Millennium Books
an imprint of E.J. Dwyer (Australia) Pty Ltd
Unit 13, Perry Park
33 Maddox Street
Alexandria NSW 2015
Phone: (02) 550 2355
Fax: (02) 519 3218

National Library of Australia
Cataloguing-in-Publication data

Morris, William, 1915–
A pocketful of stars.

ISBN 1 86429 010 2.

1. Astrology. 2. Numerology. I. Morris, Noelene. II. Title.

133.5

Cover design by Hand Graphic Design
Text design by Hand Graphic Design
Typeset in ITC Berkley Book 10/12 by DOCUPRO
Printed in Australia by Australian Print Group

10 9 8 7 6 5 4 3 2 1

98 97 96 95 94

Table of contents

Astrology

3   What Is Astrology?
5   About Your Sign
11 Looking on the Bright Side
17 Your Negative Side
23 Getting to Know You
29 What You Do Best
35 Things That Interest You
41 Getting Things Done
47 You and Friendships
53 Your Sense of Judgment
59 Work Work Work
65 In the Workplace
71 Making Money
77 Managing Your Finances
83 Romance and Relationships
89 Getting Involved
95 Romance for Two
101 Home Life
107 Family Affairs
113 Making Friends
119 Being a Friend
125 Leisure and You
131 Recreational Activities
137 Health Indications
143 Keeping Good Health
149 The Female Sunsign
155 Women and Their Partners

161 Women at Home
167 The Male Sunsign
173 Men and Their Partners
179 Men at Home
185 Sunsigns and Babies
191 The Growing Years
197 Just for the Teacher

Numerology

205 What Is Numerology?
207 General Facts About Numbers
212 Your Fundamental Qualities
218 Your Personality
223 Positive Features
228 Negative Qualities
233 Abilities of Your Number
238 Achievements
243 Interests
248 Attitudes

Astrology

· · · · · · · · · · · · · · · · · · · ·

Astrology

What is astrology?

Astrology is a science which has been studied for as long as 5000 years. Ancient records tell us it originated in Mesopotamia and was later developed in Greece. Over the years, astrology has had a profound influence on religion, science and philosophy. History is steeped in the traditions of astrology and numerology. The intangibility of these subjects has often produced sceptics but time has provided the evidence of its accuracy.

What sunsign are you?

The sun is the most important influence in astrology and it is your sunsign which reveals your basic character. There are twelve basic types of people according to the zodiac sunsign months:

Aries	21st March	to	20th April
Taurus	21st April	to	20th May

☻ A Pocketful of Stars

Gemini	21st May	to	20th June
Cancer	21st June	to	20th July
Leo	21st July	to	21st August
Virgo	22nd August	to	22nd September
Libra	23rd September	to	22nd October
Scorpio	23rd October	to	22nd November
Sagittarius	23rd November	to	20th December
Capricorn	21st December	to	19th January
Aquarius	20th January	to	18th February
Pisces	19th February	to	20th March

About Your Sign

• •

Aries

Your

◆ sign is represented by the Ram and your symbol is

◆ sign is the 1st sunsign of the zodiac and your ruling planet is Mars, the planet which symbolizes vitality, action and a pioneer spirit.

◆ sunsign represents the head and brains of Cosmic Being.

◆ most compatible zodiac signs for personal relationships are Sagittarius, Scorpio and Cancer.

Taurus

Your

◆ sign is represented by the Bull and your symbol is

◆ sign is the 2nd sunsign of the zodiac and your ruling planet is Venus, the planet of love and beauty.

◆ sunsign represents the throat of Cosmic Being.

◆ most compatible zodiac signs for personal relationships are Cancer, Leo and Capricorn.

Gemini

Your
- ◆ sign is represented by the Twins and your symbol is
- ◆ sign is the 3rd sunsign of the zodiac and your ruling planet is Mercury, symbolizing youth, relationships and change.
- ◆ sunsign represents the hands and arms of Cosmic Being.
- ◆ most compatible zodiac signs for relationships are Leo, Capricorn and Aquarius.

Cancer

Your
- ◆ sign is represented by the Crab and your symbol is
- ◆ sign is the 4th sunsign of the zodiac and you are ruled by the Moon which represents fertility, intuition and memory.
- ◆ sign represents the digestive system of Cosmic Being.
- ◆ most compatible zodiac signs are Virgo, Libra and Aquarius.

Leo

Your

- ◆ sign is represented by the King of Beasts, the Lion, and your symbol is
- ◆ sign is the 5th sunsign of the zodiac and you are ruled by the Sun, the symbol of life, expansion and authority.
- ◆ sign represents the heart and blood circulation of Cosmic Being.
- ◆ most compatible zodiac signs are Pisces, Aries and Gemini.

Virgo

Your

- ◆ sign is represented by the Virgin or Maiden and your symbol is
- ◆ sign is the 6th sunsign of the zodiac and your ruling planet is Mercury, which shows your qualities of adaptability and diplomacy.
- ◆ sign represents the digestive system and abdomen of Cosmic Being.
- ◆ most compatible zodiac signs are Capricorn, Aries and Pisces.

Libra

Your
◆ sign is represented by the Balance or Scales of Justice and your symbol is
◆ sign is the 7th sunsign of the zodiac and your ruling planet is Venus, representing your sense of justice and love of the artistic form.
◆ sign represents the kidneys and the bladder of Cosmic Being.
◆ most compatible zodiac signs are Gemini and Taurus.

Scorpio

Your
◆ sign is represented by the Scorpion and sometimes the Eagle and your symbol is
◆ sign is the 8th sunsign of the zodiac and your ruling planet is Mars, representing virility and struggle.
◆ sign represents the reproductive organs and stomach of Cosmic Being.
◆ most compatible zodiac signs for relationships are Cancer and Aquarius.

Sagittarius

Your

◆ sign is represented by the
Archer or legendary
Centaur and your symbol is
◆ sign is the 9th sunsign of the
zodiac and your ruling planet is
Jupiter, representing the law and
philosophy.
◆ sign represents the hips and thighs
as well as the artery and muscle
systems of Cosmic Being.
◆ most compatible zodiac signs are
Pisces, Cancer and Leo.

Capricorn

Your

◆ sign is represented by the
Mountain Goat and your
symbol is
◆ sign is the 10th sunsign of the
zodiac and your ruling planet is
Saturn, the planet of solitude and
trials.
◆ sign represents the knees, skeleton
and joints of Cosmic Being.
◆ most compatible zodiac signs for
relationships are Leo, Aries and
Virgo.

Aquarius

Your

◆ sign is represented by the Water Bearer and your symbol is

◆ sign is the 11th sunsign of the zodiac and your ruling planets are Saturn and Uranus, showing your desire to study and sense of brotherhood.

◆ sign represents the legs and locomotive functions of Cosmic Being.

◆ most compatible zodiac signs are Sagittarius, Taurus and Libra.

Pisces

Your

◆ sign is represented by the Fish and your symbol is

◆ sign is the 12th house of the zodiac and your ruling planet is Neptune, showing your attraction to the sea, solitary places and mysticism.

◆ sunsign represents the feet of Cosmic Being.

◆ most compatible zodiac signs for relationships are Gemini, Scorpio and Virgo.

Looking on the Bright Side

Aries

At your best you
- are quick in thought and action.
- are confident of your own ability.
- possess a pioneering spirit and enjoy a challenge.
- love talking and enjoy humor.

Keywords
- enthusiastic
- optimistic
- friendly
- independent

Taurus

At your best you
- use dignity and diplomacy where necessary.
- are a faithful and warm-hearted partner.
- enjoy simple, wholesome pleasures.
- achieve success through persistence and patience.

Keywords
- dependable
- generous
- methodical
- cheerful

Gemini

At your best you
◆ have a good sense of humor.
◆ are adaptable and believe in variety and change.
◆ are basically honest and sincere.
◆ are inventive and the originator of schemes.

Keywords
◆ active
◆ versatile
◆ observant
◆ effervescent

Cancer

At your best you
◆ are a constant person.
◆ are an individualist with a sense of your own worthiness.
◆ possess good perception, keen observation and a natural curiosity.
◆ have a humanitarian outlook.

Keywords
◆ tenacious
◆ generous
◆ knowledgeable
◆ creative

Leo

At your best you
◆ are good-hearted towards others.
◆ display self-assurance and confidence.
◆ possess a courage to overcome obstacles.
◆ get a lot of fulfillment out of living.

Keywords
◆ generous   ◆ frank
◆ enthusiastic   ◆ determined

Virgo

At your best you
◆ have very high standards in all that you do and strive to attain your ideal.
◆ seek constant self-improvement.
◆ have a clear-thinking, honest approach to life, seldom being fooled by artificiality.
◆ have an inborn respect for law and order.

Keywords
◆ honest   ◆ consciousness
◆ practical   ◆ dependable

13

Libra

At your best you
- are warm-hearted and benevolently inclined.
- have a strong sense of justice and fair play.
- are considerate, amiable and outgoing.
- have a well-developed sense of beauty.

Keywords
- diplomatic
- generous
- impartial
- pleasant

Scorpio

At your best you
- rarely give in when things go bad.
- are capable of lots of activity and appear to have boundless energy.
- are an excellent organizer and a born leader.
- are a self-reliant person with great strength of body and mind.

Keywords
- confident
- courageous
- whole-hearted
- resourceful

Sagittarius

At your best you
◆ are difficult to depress no matter what the circumstances.
◆ have respect for social order, justice and the conventions of society.
◆ are a good sport and generally well meaning in all you do.
◆ have ideals and develop your own concrete views.

Keywords
◆ optimistic
◆ jovial
◆ sociable
◆ spontaneous

Capricorn

At your best you
◆ have high principles and a strong sense of duty and obligation.
◆ are persevering and can work many problems to successful conclusions.
◆ keep your cool in emergencies.
◆ possess a keen sense of logic and reasoning.

Keywords
◆ reliable
◆ logical
◆ disciplined
◆ punctual

15

Aquarius

At your best you
- ◆ are a versatile and adaptable individualist.
- ◆ are friendly, peace-loving and dedicated to the truth.
- ◆ have keen judgment and a good reasoning ability.
- ◆ believe in trying to make the world a better place.

Keywords
- ◆ progressive
- ◆ original
- ◆ poised
- ◆ tolerant

Pisces

At your best you
- ◆ have a deep sympathy for the needy and like to be of service to others.
- ◆ possess highly developed senses and a natural understanding.
- ◆ have great fidelity and loyalty.
- ◆ take life as it comes and can rise to any heights of self-denial.

Keywords
- ◆ uncomplaining
- ◆ perceptive
- ◆ broadminded
- ◆ generous

Your Negative Side

● ●

Aries

At your worst you
◆ are a good starter but a poor finisher.
◆ don't like restrictions.
◆ lack subtlety yet resent criticism.
◆ lose your temper easily but recover quickly.

Keywords
◆ impulsive   ◆ extroverted
◆ demanding   ◆ impatient

Taurus

At your worst you
◆ have a volcanic temper.
◆ have fixed tastes and opinions.
◆ can be possessive and jealous.
◆ are easily hurt by real or imagined disloyalty.

Keywords
◆ conservative   ◆ inflexible
◆ self-centered   ◆ stubborn

Gemini

At your worst you
◆ may repel people with your moods and inconsistency.
◆ brood and worry, becoming highly strung.
◆ may be accused of being fickle because of your restlessness.
◆ are not easily satisfied.

Keyword
◆ changeable   ◆ contradictory
◆ sarcastic   ◆ superficial

Cancer

At your worst you
◆ may put up a bossy and domineering front.
◆ can be easily hurt and offended.
◆ are constantly aware of your own weaknesses.
◆ can be somewhat distant, shy and reticent.

Keywords
◆ unpredictable   ◆ pessimistic
◆ unforgiving   ◆ vain

Leo

At your worst you
◆ have hidden doubts and anxieties.
◆ are not a good judge of character.
◆ have a fiery temperament.
◆ are inclined to be extravagant and ostentatious.

Keywords
◆ arrogant
◆ impetuous
◆ outspoken
◆ overbearing

Virgo

At your worst you
◆ are vulnerable to worry about small matters and become oversensitive.
◆ are a perfectionist and expect exacting standards.
◆ are frequently misunderstood in your intentions.
◆ have a materialistic outlook and can be too analytical.

Keywords
◆ critical
◆ fastidious
◆ over-sensitive
◆ uptight

Libra

At your worst you
- are doubtful of yourself and your chances.
- can develop a strong love of pleasure and become over-indulgent.
- tend to be too easy-going and without goals.
- are too compromising and afraid to take a firm stand.

Keywords
- indecisive
- irritating
- moody
- fickle

Scorpio

At your worst you
- act without discretion or diplomacy.
- can be shrewd and contradictory.
- are a born sceptic and sometimes stubborn.
- frequently seem to be battling someone or something.

Keywords
- aggressive
- procrastinating
- conceited
- selfish

Sagittarius

At your worst you
◆ have a basic need for self-importance.
◆ make spontaneous decisions and criticisms with later regrets.
◆ are often short of tact and can be too blunt in your desire to be honest.
◆ give false compliments which you don't mean.

Keywords
◆ prejudiced ◆ restless
◆ egotistical ◆ impulsive

Capricorn

At your worst you
◆ can be uncertain due to an inferiority complex.
◆ may use speech which is too direct and critical.
◆ are too serious.
◆ worry too much and become melancholic.

Keywords
◆ uptight ◆ dogmatic
◆ apprehensive ◆ unimaginative

21

Aquarius

At your worst you
- possess subconscious forces that lead you to act in a contradictory manner.
- do not feel bound by conventional rules and regulations.
- become too tense and easily agitated.
- dislike anyone questioning you or having to submit to authority.

Keywords
- vague
- eccentric
- moody
- impatient

Pisces

At your worst you
- can be highly emotional— up or down.
- have difficulty making decisions.
- are baffling even to yourself at times.
- can become obstinate when opposed.

Keywords
- uncertain
- impressionable
- procrastinating
- melancholic

Getting to Know You

● ●

Aries

You

◆ are not bashful about voicing your opinions and usually say what you think.
◆ have the courage of your convictions and are quick to defend yourself.
◆ are sincere in your dealings with others and have a strong sense of justice.
◆ are often remembered for your fine sense of humor.

Taurus

You

◆ appear thick-skinned but hide a fragile sensitivity.
◆ are conservative by nature, tending to follow established methods.
◆ are slow to anger but, when aroused, you act "like a bull in a china shop."
◆ don't rush into things and are slow and deliberate in your ways.

Gemini

You

♦ are enthusiastic, ambitious and sensitive.
♦ have a dry wit and sparkle about you which endears you to others.
♦ tend to change your nature according to your surroundings.
♦ don't like to be left alone for long as you are a sociable personality.

Cancer

You

♦ generally don't use demonstrative behavior and are conventional and moderate in most things.
♦ are sensitive, loving, understanding and basically retiring.
♦ have alternating moods, being optimistic and energetic one moment and gloomy or depressed the next.
♦ have a kindly nature and often stop to help the person who has fallen by the wayside.

Leo

You
- ◆ have a natural pride and dignity about you and a magnetic personality.
- ◆ lose your temper quickly but generally forgive and forget easily.
- ◆ have a forceful personality and like to exercise authority.
- ◆ can be like the roaring lion or as docile as a kitten.

Virgo

You
- ◆ have a high moral code, being repelled by crudity and uncouthness.
- ◆ are basically a balanced person having a bearing which commands respect from those about you.
- ◆ believe in doing things thoroughly.
- ◆ are irritated by anything impractical or trivial.

Libra

You

◆ have an air of culture and refinement about you and good taste and dignity in matters of conduct.
◆ are keenly tuned to the thoughts and interests of others.
◆ have a subtle but persuasive manner.
◆ show a quick temper when annoyed but are quick to forgive and forget.

Scorpio

You

◆ show your individuality by your lack of concern about what others think of you.
◆ have a proud, compelling personality with a unique, magnetic attraction.
◆ rarely reveal your true self to anyone and this can puzzle those around you.
◆ have Bohemian instincts for you like to be free from restraint.

Sagittarius

You

◆ are an enthusiastic person and like to be involved in many interests.
◆ can be easily recognized by your cheerful, outspoken attitude and happy-go-lucky personality.
◆ generally love life and people.
◆ have an idealistic outlook and a strong willpower.

Capricorn

You

◆ have a quiet, reserved dignity and tend to keep your distance.
◆ have a deeply devotional nature either to a sense of duty or to religious interests.
◆ harbor secret fears and feelings of inferiority but usually put on a confident exterior.
◆ are down-to-earth and practical.

Aquarius

You
- ◆ like your independence and the right to rule yourself.
- ◆ have a decided uniqueness and originality about you.
- ◆ often perplex people as they are never quite sure what you are going to do next.
- ◆ place your confidence and hopes in the future.

Pisces

You
- ◆ are a complex and difficult person to understand and have a dual element to your personality.
- ◆ can be either positive and highly developed or negative and lazy.
- ◆ are seldom obvious in what you do so those around you have to "read between the lines."
- ◆ are intuitive with a keen insight and compassion for others.

What You Do Best

● ●

Aries

Taurus

You

◆ use your initiative and make your own decisions.

◆ possess considerable conversational ability and can converse for hours on a topic you know very little about.

◆ show your individuality in all that you do.

◆ are constantly alert to new goals and the challenge of unsolved problems.

You

◆ are popular in social and public life but work best alongside people with projective minds.

◆ are an intuitive person and this gives you an insight into people's character.

◆ can inspire loyalty and devotion in positions of leadership and responsibility.

◆ have the curious power to dominate others, even though you may not be conscious of it.

Gemini

You

- ◆ learn things easily and your active mind acquires a variety of ideas and facts.
- ◆ have an instinctive intuition which warns you of danger and alerts your observation of people's character.
- ◆ are a gifted conversationalist with a broad general knowledge.
- ◆ usually use tact and diplomacy even though your reactions are quick.

Cancer

You

- ◆ possess a natural intuition which gives a good insight into other people and their problems.
- ◆ are a constructive thinker and have a logical method of attack.
- ◆ have an inborn love of home, family, community and country.
- ◆ are very knowledgeable and quick to absorb and retain what you see.

Leo

You

◆ rarely have the ups and downs of other signs because you know how to make the most of day-to-day life.
◆ will stand up to the rights of others and the principles in which you believe.
◆ have the potential to lead and take command of a situation.
◆ are capable of coping with your share of troubles and responsibilities.

Virgo

You

◆ are not a wasteful person and often see how things can be used to their best advantage.
◆ constantly have your wits about you.
◆ are confident of your ability even though you prefer to remain in the background and follow set routines.
◆ have the ability to dissect and to simplify problems and try to improve yourself through education and hard work.

Libra

You
- ◆ seldom do things without having regard for the consequences.
- ◆ have the ability to re-adjust your thinking on all things around you.
- ◆ can be a smooth and subtle talker and well able to defend yourself.
- ◆ are a good sport and can take your share of disappointment.

Scorpio

You
- ◆ have strong willpower which, if properly directed, will lead you to great things.
- ◆ were born with highly developed emotions for which you may seek outlets.
- ◆ are a most resourceful person who can make the most of circumstances.
- ◆ can fight your own battles and even thrive on problems.

Sagittarius

You

- ◆ have the ability to think and act quickly and to recover quickly from setbacks.
- ◆ have a good sense of humor and know how to phrase things effectively.
- ◆ possess a good conversational ability and actually enjoy a good argument.
- ◆ are a practical person capable of positive action and persistent effort.

Capricorn

You

- ◆ are a persistent person and seldom deviate from your goals once you have made up your mind.
- ◆ have the ability to gain and hold a position of responsibility.
- ◆ have a logical and practical mind which will solve many a problem when others have given up.
- ◆ have good organizational ability and enjoy a challenge.

33

Aquarius

You

◆ are sensitive to the attitudes and welfare of others and have a natural ability to understand people.

◆ can use your imaginative ability to review your progress and develop new ideas.

◆ are able to pay attention to details more than most and have keen powers of observation and analysis.

◆ have an excellent memory when you concentrate and can be quick to acquire knowledge.

Pisces

You

◆ are a born actor.

◆ can be exacting and work earnestly to achieve what you believe to be your duty.

◆ have a duality about your abilities, being both practical and painstaking as well as mysterious and imaginative.

◆ often rely on your instincts to influence you and you possess a perception which keeps you wise in the ways of life.

Things That Interest You

Aries

You

◆ enjoy your freedom to mingle with people and exchange ideas.
◆ often create new ideas and schemes.
◆ are adventurous by nature and are seldom afraid to take a risk.
◆ enjoy tackling difficult problems.

Taurus

You

◆ take great pride in your possessions and enjoy creating an attractive home.
◆ have a taste and appreciation for beauty and harmony.
◆ are most influenced by your appetite and passions.
◆ are a practical person and are creative with your hands.

Gemini

You

◆ become restless when life is dull and you hate to be in a rut.
◆ have a desire to live a romantic and picturesque life.
◆ mix well socially and like to move from group to group.
◆ are curious and receptive to new subjects.

Cancer

You

◆ have a restless need for excitement in your life.
◆ love your home life and are well-suited to the domestic scene.
◆ will fight for what you believe is right without seeking personal reward.
◆ enjoy important ceremonies because of their impressiveness, and are interested in public affairs.

Leo

You

◆ enjoy a challenge and like excitement and adventure in your life.

◆ have the ability to enjoy the present to the full and do not like to be hurried.

◆ like grandeur and enjoy your material possessions.

◆ love to be in the spotlight and thoroughly enjoy being the center of attention.

Virgo

You

◆ are fussy about your personal appearance and like to look neat and tidy.

◆ are fond of intellectual pursuits such as lectures, entertainment, the arts, reading, music and making collections.

◆ constantly desire to improve yourself as your own achievements are important to you.

◆ have a high regard for all your possessions and like a place for everything and to have everything in its place.

Libra

You

◆ show a genuine interest in the injustices of humankind.

◆ will probably make the most of your creative ability to further your achievements and ambitions.

◆ are interested in organizations connected with culture, beauty and the humanities.

◆ understand the need for laughter, music, order and pleasant surroundings.

Scorpio

You

◆ are constantly in search of inner values and seek your own philosophy on life.

◆ enjoy a good argument, especially when you are the winner.

◆ are fascinated by secrets, the mystical, the curious and the struggle of life and death.

◆ have a love of nature and enjoy sensual experiences.

Sagittarius

You
- ◆ show an interest in the welfare of others and often support community activities.
- ◆ are a born adventurer, speculator, traveller and explorer.
- ◆ love talking and enjoy opportunities where you can express your opinions.
- ◆ have a love of change in your life, especially a change of scenery.

Capricorn

You
- ◆ desire the good things in life, but in moderation.
- ◆ are keen to be a success in life and are willing to work hard to achieve this.
- ◆ have a strong sense of artistic appreciation.
- ◆ have a thirst for knowledge.

Aquarius

You
- ◆ are generally involved in some activity for public good.
- ◆ have a great love of humanity and a fascination for the hidden forces of nature.
- ◆ have an insatiable curiosity about the sciences and are attracted to music, philosophy and literature.
- ◆ are frequently more interested in helping others than you are in helping yourself.

Pisces

You
- ◆ support things you believe will make the world a better place.
- ◆ are attracted to mysterious things and may shut yourself off from others to enjoy the solitude.
- ◆ love beauty and have a fine sense of humor.
- ◆ like to lend an ear to troubled acquaintances along the way.

Getting Things Done
• •

Aries

Avoid

◆ accomplishing very little as a result of doing too many things.

◆ cramped living and working conditions as these retard your achievements.

◆ taking unnecessary risks: "Look before you leap."

◆ achieving your ambitions at the expense of home and family.

Taurus

Avoid

◆ others shifting their share of responsibility onto you.

◆ hurried decisions as you are not disposed to haphazard methods.

◆ a life of hustle and bustle because you are the happiest in quiet and peaceful places.

◆ becoming complacent with your own comfort and ease.

Gemini

Avoid

◆ being so versatile in your undertakings that you have difficulty in persevering.

◆ your inclination towards nervous unrest and indecision.

◆ being neglectful of your duties because you dislike monotony.

◆ becoming bored, as this leaves time for moods.

Cancer

Avoid

◆ trying to get things done in a rush.

◆ daydreaming about past events and being retrospective too often.

◆ the inclination to copy rather than being original.

◆ developing a lazy inertia as you wait for life to happen.

Leo

Avoid

◆ being carried away by enthusiasm and optimism of the moment.
◆ becoming highly strung through involving yourself in too much activity.
◆ sulking and losing interest in your work if you are not receiving the appreciation you believe you deserve.
◆ your inclination to rush about and miss attention to detail.

Virgo

Avoid

◆ a disorderly environment as this prevents you from working efficiently.
◆ constant demands on yourself to achieve perfection.
◆ noisy environments as these are upsetting to your nature.
◆ doing several things at once as you work best doing one thing at a time.

Libra

Avoid
- neglecting your own true talents and becoming easily discouraged.
- being uncertain of your own ideas and actions.
- allowing your love of peace and harmony to hinder your enthusiasm and dilute your ambitions.
- being so desirous of a life of ease and pleasure that you become untidy in your habits.

Scorpio

Avoid
- expecting to achieve quick promotion and prestige.
- becoming restless when life is proceeding smoothly.
- the possibility of losing your job because of your lack of tact with people.
- acting without giving consideration to another's point of view.

Sagittarius

Avoid
- ◆ wearing yourself out by your restless, unrelenting activity.
- ◆ making promises which you either forget or have little intention of carrying out.
- ◆ acting impatiently and impulsively without considering the consequences.
- ◆ being ignorant of your own shortcomings and learn to recognize your own weaknesses.

Capricorn

Avoid
- ◆ your inclination to be pessimistic rather than optimistic.
- ◆ using the weak points of others to your own advantage.
- ◆ being too slow to adapt to new ideas.
- ◆ placing too many restrictions on yourself as this can make you difficult to live with.

Aquarius

Avoid
- giving way to daydreaming instead of employing your time more constructively.
- keeping to yourself too much and being too self-contained.
- convincing yourself that all is well when in fact it isn't.
- letting yourself become confused and uncertain when presented with new situations.

Pisces

Avoid
- being so satisfied with your dreams that you never make them a reality.
- being hesitant and waiting to be asked for your opinions.
- being reserved about becoming involved in things around you.
- neglecting your responsibilities if life becomes complicated.

You and Friendships

Aries

Avoid
- ◆ talking too much about yourself and your plans.
- ◆ hurting the feelings of others with your forthright speech.
- ◆ neglecting those around you who should receive more attention.
- ◆ dominating your marital partner and friends.

Taurus

Avoid
- ◆ losing your temper as it may be harmful to your relationships and ambitions.
- ◆ becoming fixed in your thinking and viewpoints.
- ◆ being too emotionally sensitive.
- ◆ being slow to react as others may think you lack animation.

Gemini

Avoid
- ◆ an inclination to become easily irritated by trifles.
- ◆ resenting advice given in good faith.
- ◆ being dissatisfied with your lot as you become difficult to live with.
- ◆ a restlessness which may affect your progress and perseverance.

Cancer

Avoid
- ◆ giving the impression that you are difficult to approach.
- ◆ displaying your obstinate streak.
- ◆ your inclination to unconsciously absorb the attitudes and habits of those close to you.
- ◆ a tendency to be shy by concentrating on your talents.

Leo

Avoid

◆ imposing your will on others.
◆ bearing a grudge when your pride is hurt.
◆ an involvement in quarrels as you are likely to say things which you regret.
◆ assuming a snobbish attitude without due reason.

Virgo

Avoid

◆ becoming so involved in your work that you neglect the social side of your life.
◆ making "mountains out of molehills."
◆ thinking your ways of doing things are superior to others.
◆ weakening a relationship by your fault-finding.

Libra

Avoid

- ◆ becoming weak and compliant for the sake of keeping the peace.
- ◆ a tendency to want to hide from the realities of life.
- ◆ becoming melancholy if conditions aren't to your liking or making yourself miserable by worrying.
- ◆ any vain desire to be noticed, praised or flattered.

Scorpio

Avoid

- ◆ bearing a grudge and being unforgiving.
- ◆ considering yourself superior to others.
- ◆ losing patience if things are not going as planned.
- ◆ your inclination to be abrupt, irritable and contradictory.

Sagittarius

Avoid
- ◆ flaring up when you are crossed.
- ◆ having biased viewpoints and try to consider the opinions and feelings of others.
- ◆ talking too much and sounding off about high ideals.
- ◆ having preconceived ideas and strong aversions to people or establishments.

Capricorn

Avoid
- ◆ becoming annoyed over little things.
- ◆ being aloof from social contact.
- ◆ feeling gloomy or even vengeful when you believe you are unjustly treated.
- ◆ acting in a superior manner and try to be more at ease.

Aquarius

Avoid

◆ speaking unpleasantly when you are in a bad mood.
◆ being quick to form opinions and being stubborn about changing your mind.
◆ being condescending towards others.
◆ staying offended and unforgiving as you will have difficulty regaining the confidence and friendship of others.

Pisces

Avoid

◆ making those around you unhappy because of your moods.
◆ becoming over-anxious about your life and worrying too much.
◆ isolating yourself without first telling others that you need to be alone for a while.
◆ thinking that people don't understand you and persecuting yourself.

Your Sense of Judgment

● ●

Aries

Avoid
◆ assessing people quickly by external appearances.
◆ being easily distracted by side issues.
◆ being impatient with yourself.
◆ acting on impulse as it may cause disillusionment or financial loss.

Taurus

Avoid
◆ making decisions and judgments according to your mood of the moment.
◆ being cornered into making quick decisions as you need time to think.
◆ impulsive outbursts where you disregard the consequences.
◆ being influenced too much by the opinions and feelings of others.

Gemini

Avoid

- ◆ recalling an insult before a kindness.
- ◆ being susceptible to flattery and its lures.
- ◆ interjecting in others' conversations.
- ◆ over-analyzing your problems as this may only cause you to think you are inadequate.

Cancer

Avoid

- ◆ underestimating yourself and lowering your own self-esteem.
- ◆ letting others take advantage of your sympathetic nature.
- ◆ taking a joke the wrong way.
- ◆ being constantly concerned about what others think of you.

Leo

Avoid
- ◆ being misled by flattery and false compliments.
- ◆ your desire to be the center of attention for you have an enormous ego.
- ◆ being too authoritarian and inflexible.
- ◆ making promises which you may not be able to keep.

Virgo

Avoid
- ◆ being intolerant of people whose standards and attitudes may vary from yours.
- ◆ driving yourself to emotional illness with your unyielding ambition and pride.
- ◆ a belief that all things should be straightforward and orderly.
- ◆ seeing a narrow view of things rather than taking a broader perspective.

Libra

Avoid
- expecting too much out of life and being disappointed if things do not all go your way.
- those times when you are tempted to deliberately deceive others.
- falling victim to the opportunist who plays on your desire for recognition and flattery.
- being hesitant for your first impressions are usually correct.

Scorpio

Avoid
- turning your home into an unhappy place because of your autocratic manner.
- becoming a law-breaker as a result of making your own rules about what is right and wrong.
- making fun of others.
- allowing your desire for physical excesses to overpower your self-control.

Sagittarius

Avoid
- breaking in on others' conversations.
- your tendency to exaggerate whether out of enthusiasm, high ideals or your ego.
- a lack of subtlety with your jokes.
- speaking contemptuously to others on the pretext that you are doing it for their own good.

Capricorn

Avoid
- having preconceived ideas and prejudices.
- an overdeveloped sense of economy.
- reasoning according to your personal feelings and seeing things only from your point of view.
- being overly conscious of your prestige and status.

Aquarius

Avoid
◆ reacting quickly with your emotions before you have had a chance to analyze a situation logically.
◆ showing resentment towards authority.
◆ blaming others when things go wrong instead of searching for your own inefficiency.
◆ stirring up dissatisfaction amongst those around you for this is a negative and destructive quality.

Pisces

Avoid
◆ cutting yourself off from others when you feel hurt.
◆ a stubbornness which prevents you from saying sorry or admitting that you're wrong.
◆ becoming an easy target for people with a hard luck story.
◆ confusing people, for they find it difficult to know whether you really mean what you say.

Work Work Work

· ·

Aries

You

◆ have a strong drive to achieve and be successful.

◆ are a forward-looking person and usually keep abreast of new developments.

◆ often seek new fields to conquer as you are a person of action and inventiveness.

◆ are an excellent starter, but don't always finish if your interest is not sustained.

Taurus

You

◆ get through plenty of work without tiring and bore in until a job is satisfactorily completed.

◆ appear slow to others but in fact you are just being sure.

◆ are capable of carrying on calmly under pressure.

◆ are willing to work hard for your success and material comforts.

Gemini

You
- ◆ have an insatiable curiosity and can be involved in many things at once.
- ◆ should try to achieve immediate goals as these will add purpose to your daily life.
- ◆ are quick to assess the advantages of new ideas.
- ◆ are usually at your best when working under pressure.

Cancer

You
- ◆ are a loyal employee if treated fairly.
- ◆ know how to persevere and can work successfully on routine business because of your patience.
- ◆ can take the initiative to lead others and be successful.
- ◆ are a dependable, conscientious worker and produce positive results without boasting of your achievements.

Leo

You

◆ have the capacity for hard work and an ambitious drive which leads you to higher positions.

◆ are best suited to a job in which you can exercise some authority and responsibility.

◆ are more successful in general planning and supervision than in detailed work.

◆ seldom give in to failure as you strive to be successful.

Virgo

You

◆ work longer but slower than most people as you pay attention to detail.

◆ would probably be a specialist in your field, devoting much time and study to it.

◆ set yourself high standards and experience great satisfaction when you reach your goals.

◆ can persevere with your work, offering a unique combination of persistence and nervous energy.

Libra

You

◆ are flexible in your work capacity and adjustable to change.

◆ can be counted on to do the right thing at the right time and seldom oppose authority unless an injustice is involved.

◆ may appear to be conservative and slow about making decisions.

◆ get on well with others and are suited to partnership ventures.

Scorpio

You

◆ possess quick intellectual abilities and the natural ability to grasp the main points.

◆ will try to work out new or quicker methods of doing your work and achieving your aims.

◆ are capable of prolonged and sustained efforts once you have made up your mind to do it.

◆ have good powers of concentration which enable you to persevere in adverse conditions.

Sagittarius

You
◆ like work in which you can express yourself and show the extent of your capacities.
◆ are quick to evaluate set tasks and can carry them to a successful conclusion.
◆ are able to inspire confidence in others with your self-reliance and bright personality.
◆ do not like being tied to detailed work.

Capricorn

You
◆ can be trusted with responsibility and work cooperatively with others.
◆ work best in controlled and orderly surroundings.
◆ are a hard worker, having stability and staying power.
◆ are seldom imaginative or original in your ideas and are more successful when applying the ideas of others.

Aquarius

You

- ◆ are capable of working on large and challenging projects.
- ◆ enjoy keeping busy and are seldom idle as you don't believe in wasting time.
- ◆ are able to work quickly and efficiently and make helpful suggestions for improvements.
- ◆ have the capacity to be a success through your perseverance, regardless of your educational qualifications.

Pisces

You

- ◆ can combine the practical side together with the theory.
- ◆ are an adaptable person and adjust quickly to changes.
- ◆ work well with both your employers and co-workers.
- ◆ like to receive encouragement which spurs your efforts.

In the Workplace

● ●

Aries

You

◆ would be wise to avoid monotonous work but rather seek an occupation which involves your imagination and individuality.

◆ work best if you organize your own work routine.

◆ dislike restricted situations which will slowly extinguish your energies and inspirations.

◆ are usually pleasant to work for, but remember to praise a job well done.

Taurus

You

◆ work best when you are motivated and stimulated by a positive force.

◆ are suited to long assignments as you have the perseverance and hardiness to complete them.

◆ work best to established routines.

◆ may miss out on good deals as a result of your dislike of change.

Gemini

You

◆ work well with others but are generally happier when working on your own.

◆ find it difficult to sit down to continuous work and should avoid long, drawn-out projects.

◆ like to be busy with more than one thing and may even have two jobs.

◆ don't work well in a job which doesn't interest you.

Cancer

You

◆ work well if you like what you are doing and should never lose sight of your ultimate goal.

◆ can work well with people and are sympathetic to those in need.

◆ probably approach a task gradually rather than directly and are quite capable of waiting for long-term results.

◆ have the ability to initiate your own success.

Leo

You

◆ prefer to be your own boss rather than have people tell you what to do.

◆ have a bright personality and optimistic outlook which enlivens the morale of those around you.

◆ are usually successful by degrees rather than becoming an overnight success.

◆ should avoid a desk job involving details, for you need to be active.

Virgo

You

◆ are likely to rise steadily rather than be an overnight success.

◆ are happiest when applying your ability and talent to good use.

◆ dislike loose ends at the completion of any work.

◆ generally like to be left alone to work at your own pace.

Libra

You

◆ work better with people than with products.

◆ have a natural tact which allows you to get on well with others at work.

◆ are not suited to strenuous or untidy occupations.

◆ are a great advocate of people working in harmony with each other and with nature.

Scorpio

You

◆ enjoy work which presents a challenge to you.

◆ dislike being closely supervised or having restrictions placed on you at work.

◆ are seldom affected by the physical surroundings at your place of work.

◆ should guard against allowing your idealism or religious beliefs to affect your career.

Sagittarius

You
◆ are generally considerate of your workmates and will stand up for them if you believe an injustice has been done.
◆ generally seek promotion in your chosen occupation.
◆ dislike restraint in your freedom of movement and could become depressed by sedentary work.
◆ are inclined to make hasty decisions which could spoil your chances of success.

Capricorn

You
◆ have a strong desire to maintain a good reputation and rarely make a fool of yourself.
◆ usually have a desire to be in a position of authority.
◆ strive for your ideals and appreciate recognition of your efforts and worth.
◆ may be prevented from reaching your goals by your own inflexibility and intolerance.

Aquarius

You

◆ need to find work which tests your intellect and ingenuity.

◆ are seldom interested in routine work but prefer the chance of doing something more challenging.

◆ should try to find a job in which you can express your philosophical outlook and can extend your creative talents.

◆ usually need the assistance of others to bring your ideas into a practical reality.

Pisces

You

◆ like variety in your work for you are a flexible person.

◆ enjoy employment which stimulates your imagination.

◆ are capable of fluency and correctness of detail when interested in your work.

◆ have a genuine desire to be of service to others.

Making Money

● ●

Aries

You

- ◆ are prepared to work hard for your money.
- ◆ should avoid "get rich quick" schemes.
- ◆ have a good earning capacity but seldom amass a fortune.
- ◆ are attracted towards speculation and gambling because of your adventurous nature.

Taurus

You

- ◆ seldom take monetary risks.
- ◆ have a lucky streak and often become a winner when you do take a chance.
- ◆ can be so ambitious to make money that you take little time off to relax.
- ◆ should invest some money in practical prospects during favorable financial periods.

Gemini

You

- ◆ often look for ways to better your financial situation.
- ◆ like to achieve financial gain by scheming and clever planning.
- ◆ are not the kind of person who is willing to work for nothing.
- ◆ are not easily fooled and are seldom taken for a ride in monetary matters.

Cancer

You

- ◆ can successfully apply your intuition to financial and business matters.
- ◆ may have the urge to speculate and gamble but should avoid the "get rich quick" schemes.
- ◆ have a good earning capacity.
- ◆ have the capacity to accumulate money or property through wise investment.

Leo

You
- have an instinct and natural talent for making money.
- are inspired by better financial opportunities, particularly those gained through more prestigious positions.
- may get carried away with gambling and throw caution to the wind.
- were born under a sign which indicates financial security and even wealth.

Virgo

You
- rarely take financial risks but are likely to take up a secure investment.
- work hard for your financial gains and enjoy acquiring money.
- regard work as the natural solution to any financial crisis.
- may gather a modest fortune by diligent work.

Libra

You
- ◆ are not overly concerned with making money or piling up wealth.
- ◆ will probably go through considerable sums of money in your lifetime.
- ◆ need to be more thrifty while on your way to success.
- ◆ can be financially successful if married to a practical partner.

Scorpio

You
- ◆ have a shrewd eye and are quick to see financial advantages.
- ◆ usually benefit financially in partnerships both in business and in marriage.
- ◆ have the willpower and determination to get where you want to go to improve your financial status.
- ◆ generally are lucky with money though you would be wise not to gamble unless you are prepared to lose.

Sagittarius

You
- ◆ are generally materially successful in your lifetime.
- ◆ may take risks in order to gain large profits.
- ◆ are intuitive in many matters concerning money and you will find this ability useful if you use it wisely.
- ◆ have a happy-go-lucky attitude to money even when your luck is down.

Capricorn

You
- ◆ seldom take a chance on your luck and rarely gamble except on a sure thing.
- ◆ will make profit from investments in real estate, established firms, government bonds and stocks.
- ◆ have a determination to succeed and this will see you through a financial crisis.
- ◆ are ambitious in your desire to get ahead in your employment so as to improve your financial status.

Aquarius

You

◆ sometimes let financial
opportunities slip by.
◆ are not usually successful in
speculative ventures and should
avoid "get rick quick" schemes.
◆ may show little ambition if you are
financially well-off.
◆ are always convinced by figures.

Pisces

You

◆ should consider wise investment
on a regular savings basis.
◆ should be consciously aware that
you can be used by others who
play on your sympathy and
generosity.
◆ may earn money by fascinating and
extraordinary occupations.
◆ would be well advised to push
forward into positions which are
due to you and will benefit you
financially.

Managing Your Finances

● ●

Aries

You
◆ are inclined to be a generous spender and tend to live for the moment.
◆ like money for it gives you a lot of pleasure.
◆ don't balance a budget too well.
◆ should try to be thrifty and build on your reserves.

Taurus

You
◆ appreciate the things money can do for you.
◆ resent being over-charged or short-changed.
◆ understand the value of money and have good money sense.
◆ view money as your security and means of comfort.

Gemini

You

◆ like money for the security it gives you.
◆ are generally cautious in money matters but others may think you are tight.
◆ can be easily influenced in money matters by someone you love.
◆ occasionally do something foolish with money.

Cancer

You

◆ can be thrifty, even frugal, with your money.
◆ have a need for the security which money brings you.
◆ are discreetly generous with the things that money can buy.
◆ are honest when dealing with money and expect others to be the same.

Leo

You

◆ are usually generous with your cash, especially if you are well-off.
◆ like to feel the success of acquiring luxuries and expensive things around you.
◆ are inclined to be impulsive at times with your money.
◆ are not generally careless with the management of your money for secretly you fear being poor.

Virgo

You

◆ are careful with your money and save diligently.
◆ are generous with your money when you are well-off but can be reluctant to part with your hard-earned cash.
◆ are a good credit risk as you guard against over-committing yourself.
◆ are not happy about buying something if you don't get your full money's worth.

Libra

You
- do not usually retain your money for too long because of your generosity and tendency to overspend.
- very rarely hoard money for you enjoy spending it on things which make life pleasant.
- can be shrewd in money matters and surprisingly exacting in financial dealings when necessary.
- probably spend considerable sums of money on social activities, entertaining and artistic pursuits.

Scorpio

You
- are unpredictable in money matters for you can scrimp and save or, alternatively, can be unnecessarily extravagant.
- should be realistic about the money you can spend without straining the budget.
- can be honest or dishonest with money depending on your own ethics and rules.
- enjoy money and the pleasures it brings.

Sagittarius

You
- ◆ are seldom mean or petty with your finances.
- ◆ should avoid allowing the bills to pile up while you spend money on frills.
- ◆ can be extravagant in your spending on good wine, food, clothes, first class travel, social and sporting activities.
- ◆ need to pay attention to the smaller daily expenditures for this could be the area in which you are careless with money.

Capricorn

You
- ◆ are a thrifty person who shops wisely and drives a hard bargain.
- ◆ can live frugally and usually put aside a nest egg for a rainy day.
- ◆ should guard against becoming miserly in your desire to accumulate money.
- ◆ can be generous and charitable or, alternatively, be stingy with your money when worried about financial burdens.

Aquarius

You

◆ are not particularly interested in money although you are practical in your use of it.
◆ use your money as a means to an end.
◆ are not always as careful in your financial affairs as you should be.
◆ are neither a spendthrift nor a miser in money matters.

Pisces

You

◆ realise that money is the main means by which you can fulfil your ideals and aims.
◆ can be influenced by the one you love in managing financial matters.
◆ dread poverty or lean times and this may curb your generous nature.
◆ can be a spendthrift during changes of mood.

Romance and Relationships

● ●

Aries

You
- ◆ may leap impulsively and intensely into romantic situations too soon.
- ◆ would be wise to marry later than most to ensure emotional maturity and marital fidelity.
- ◆ should marry someone who shares your natural enthusiasm in things which interest you.
- ◆ generally make a loyal partner though not always easy to live with and certainly never a bore.

Taurus

You
- ◆ need a partner who appreciates your ability to manage finances, provide good food and enjoy artistic pursuits.
- ◆ are likely to have only one true love during your lifetime.
- ◆ show stability in your devotion to your partner.
- ◆ are more affectionate than passionate.

Gemini

You

- ◆ are attracted to people who have an independent attitude similar to your own.
- ◆ are likely to find that your love life is complex owing to your Gemini duality.
- ◆ like some freedom even though you are tied to commitments.
- ◆ can be misunderstood by your partner when mental problems make you physically indifferent.

Cancer

You

- ◆ set high standards for your partner, preferring to go without love than settle for second best.
- ◆ are prepared to make sacrifices to ensure that your relationship is successful.
- ◆ may need to loosen up so as to have as few inhibitions as possible in your romantic relations.
- ◆ should guard against giving too much attention to your children and thus neglecting your partner.

Leo

You

◆ should guard against marrying a person who has temporarily changed their personality to harmonize with your own.

◆ would be wise not to seek a partner who can be jealous, possessive or doubtful of your love.

◆ are selective in your choice of partner and are prepared to wait for someone who lives up to your ideals.

◆ achieve inner serenity when you are contented with your relationship.

Virgo

You

◆ derive greatest pleasure from intellectual compatibility which in turn provides you with emotional security.

◆ are easily influenced by the ones you love.

◆ can be unfairly suspicious of your partner.

◆ should take care not to lack romantic affection, as this may lead to misunderstandings.

Libra

You

◆ will more than likely begin your romantic attachments at an early age.

◆ have a great need to find your ideal partner for love can be your main reason for living.

◆ need to keep in mind that true love involves equal giving and taking.

◆ are noted for your affectionate nature but should guard against feelings of jealousy.

Scorpio

You

◆ belong to the zodiac house most influenced by physical love.

◆ are attracted to the physical attributes of your partner.

◆ need a partner who can satisfy your physical desires as well as your intellectual capabilities.

◆ may be inclined to form secret attachments and would be wise to exercise discretion.

Sagittarius

You

◆ are not easy to hold in a close partnership for your high-spirited love of life is hard to keep up with.

◆ should avoid the home-loving domestic partner who does not enjoy outside interests or you will both spend a lot of time alone.

◆ like having your independence even when tied up with family obligations.

◆ need a partner who listens to your troubles and gives you companionship and understanding.

Capricorn

You

◆ need a partner who can fulfil your necessity to have companionship.

◆ should be careful not to take your partner for granted once the honeymoon is over.

◆ value your relationship for the security it gives you.

◆ are reserved in your romantic relations.

Aquarius

You
- ◆ become more strongly attached to your partner as time passes.
- ◆ rarely let your affections stray once you commit to a relationship.
- ◆ need the affections of an intellectual partner who will be a devoted companion to you.
- ◆ are not inclined to be the boss of the household but neither will you be subjected to another's directions.

Pisces

You
- ◆ desire to have a happy harmonious marriage for this gives you the emotional security you need.
- ◆ need someone who is understanding of both your strengths and weaknesses.
- ◆ like to be shown gentle signs of love and affection.
- ◆ are at most times the ideal mate but, as in all partnerships, there are storms to be weathered.

Getting Involved

• •

Aries

You

◆ are capable of falling in love at first sight.

◆ are affectionate, tender and inclined to passion.

◆ often feel strangely alone despite a permanent union.

◆ need a partner who gives you stability, serenity and understanding.

Taurus

You

◆ are usually direct in expressing your feelings.

◆ are sometimes undemonstrative and lacking in an outward display of warmth.

◆ require reassurance and emotional security from your partner.

◆ can be possessive and jealous, demanding your partner's complete attention.

Gemini

You
- ◆ long for understanding and affection which you don't always find.
- ◆ like to give and to be given affection.
- ◆ change your affections depending on your mental attitudes.
- ◆ need to adapt to married life especially by controlling your moods.

Cancer

You
- ◆ seldom display your affections in a demonstrative or outgoing way.
- ◆ have a great need for tenderness and attention but should avoid being selfish in these demands.
- ◆ are inclined to become morose when your partner is absent.
- ◆ can sometimes become over-whelmed by the feeling that you are not really loved.

Leo

You

◆ are a passionate person and you are probably quite an accomplished lover.
◆ enjoy the sensual pleasures of life.
◆ can become emotional in love and may go to unusual lengths to obtain satisfaction.
◆ are quite sentimental and like to give gifts as well as receive them.

Virgo

You

◆ usually show your love in practical ways as you believe duty and service are important.
◆ go to great lengths to maintain your happiness.
◆ are attracted to those who need help owing to the sympathetic side of your nature.
◆ do not easily overcome the hurt of a broken romance.

Libra

You

◆ are happiest when your emotions are aroused and charged.

◆ are inclined to be sentimental and easily moved.

◆ are by nature a passionate person although this is often concealed beneath a poised veneer.

◆ can be so in love with someone in the beginning that you fail to see the true personality and forget to judge impartially.

Scorpio

You

◆ love with great passion but often combine your affections with possessiveness.

◆ are a lost soul without someone to love.

◆ may hide your feelings and this can be confusing to your partner.

◆ hate to be scorned in love.

Sagittarius

You
- ◆ waste no time in expressing your feelings when you believe you have found the right partner.
- ◆ have a direct and positive way of showing your love.
- ◆ may be a little naive in matters of love and this could cause you disappointment at times.
- ◆ should take care not to hurt your partner's feelings with thoughtless words during moments alone.

Capricorn

You
- ◆ are generally ruled by your head not your heart in romantic matters.
- ◆ will return affection with affection.
- ◆ have calculated rather than spontaneous emotional responses.
- ◆ love deeply but believe your actions speak louder than words.

Aquarius

You

♦ will be sincere and affectionate in your marriage as long as you can have your moments of privacy and freedom of movement.
♦ are basically a sensitive person and can be easily hurt.
♦ can be so in love with love that your heart rules your head when selecting a partner.
♦ often conceal your real feelings.

Pisces

You

♦ feel deeply and, if well mated, you give your love for good.
♦ have a strong need for emotional reassurance.
♦ are romantic by nature and are sincere in your affections.
♦ can be completely immersed in the being of your loved one.

Romance for Two

· ·

Aries

You

- ◆ are an intense lover, but when the fire goes out you are off hunting again.
- ◆ believe in sacrificing much for your love and you are usually faithful once committed.
- ◆ enjoy attention, praise and flattery and like to hear the submissive "yes".
- ◆ sometimes dislike the restrictions that a committed relationship places on your independence and personal freedom.

Taurus

You

- ◆ are faithful once in love.
- ◆ make a considerate and generous partner.
- ◆ believe that marriage is two people giving completely of themselves.
- ◆ can show a mean streak in your nature if all does not go well at home.

Gemini

You

- are generally easy to get along with and are willing to make compromises.
- enjoy flirting and usually have little difficulty making conquests.
- set your own moral code on sexual matters.
- expect your partner to be an intellectual equal as well as appreciative and attentive.

Cancer

You

- find life a dull existence without romance.
- sympathize strongly with your partner's needs.
- treat love seriously and are devoted to your chosen partner.
- look on love as a means of protection from the world.

Leo

You
- ◆ are usually faithful in love as constancy is important to you.
- ◆ have a strong need to care for someone and be cared for in return.
- ◆ like your partner to live up to your own set of ideals otherwise you become quickly disillusioned.
- ◆ should regard your romantic life as an equal give and take relationship.

Virgo

You
- ◆ do not feign affection if it is not there.
- ◆ like to keep to established routines and maintain some independence even in a relationship.
- ◆ are protective of the one you love.
- ◆ are determined to preserve your happiness once married.

Libra

You
- are a sentimental person and like to keep souvenirs of your romance.
- dislike being single as you enjoy sharing your interests.
- endeavor to be an understanding partner.
- usually know a lot about romantic matters, for love is important to you.

Scorpio

You
- like to know that your partner's attraction is for you alone.
- are sexually orientated in many things that you do.
- may cause disappointment in your marriage through indiscretion.
- are seldom tolerant of weaknesses in the one you love.

Sagittarius

You

◆ set high standards for your partner and have to accept your lot if your ideals are not reached.

◆ can hurt the feelings of your loved one and create misunderstanding by your unsparing wit.

◆ often want things your own way without considering the two-way importance of a relationship.

◆ are philosophically inclined, even in your romantic attachments.

Capricorn

You

◆ are generally sincere and constant in aspects of love.

◆ are usually emotionally restrained and reserved and seldom impressed by emotional reactions.

◆ could use marriage for your material gain or social prestige.

◆ maintain your self-discipline even in matters of romance.

Aquarius

You

- ◆ should keep in mind that you can be more in love with the idea of love than actually loving.
- ◆ will not allow yourself to be totally absorbed or possessed by love.
- ◆ believe in holding onto your sense of freedom even when deeply in love.
- ◆ seldom do anything to cause discord in your relationship; in fact, you make one of the best partners.

Pisces

You

- ◆ can puzzle your mate with your changing attitudes.
- ◆ should avoid becoming possessive of your partner.
- ◆ should avoid making scenes and losing your temper as this can only damage your relationship.
- ◆ are generally faithful and sincere though not always an ardent lover.

Home Life

Aries

You

◆ usually live in the city as you like to live near activity and excitement.
◆ need the stability of owning your own home.
◆ like to have things clean and tidy and get depressed in shabby and cramped surroundings.
◆ like to be fashionable as well as have a comfortable home in a casual setting.

Taurus

You

◆ have a hospitable home that makes visitors feel welcome.
◆ seek a happy, orderly home life.
◆ like to be surrounded by familiar and comfortable things.
◆ need plenty of space around you and your own garden area.

Gemini

You

◆ like to live in a friendly neighbourhood within easy access to community facilities.
◆ desire to achieve contentment and peace in your home environment.
◆ like changes in your home and use your resourcefulness to make these.
◆ enjoy fixing things and making improvements around the home.

Cancer

You

◆ are a great home-lover as you are quite domestic by nature.
◆ like to establish yourself and are most reluctant to leave.
◆ probably have lots of keepsakes stored away and you are usually sentimental about old family things.
◆ like unpretentious colors, a quiet relaxing decor, lots of storage space and a nice garden.

Leo

You

◆ like all the comforts that your money can buy.

◆ regard your home as your castle in which you like to relax in comfort.

◆ like to show others the efforts you have put into your home and are delighted with favorable comments.

◆ enjoy entertaining at home and you make a fine host.

Virgo

You

◆ are a home-loving person who likes to be surrounded by the things you enjoy.

◆ are methodical with your domestic duties but repetition may upset your nervous system.

◆ like a functional home which is easy to clean and maintain.

◆ are sensitive to your surroundings and need a harmonious home atmosphere to maintain your good humor.

Libra

You
- ◆ use your understanding nature to create an aura of contentment in your home.
- ◆ like to have beautiful things around you and your home often gives the impression of gracious living.
- ◆ should avoid buying a home in a noisy or untidy environment as these are abhorrent to you.
- ◆ may have a little untidiness about your home at times but beneath the clutter is a sense of order.

Scorpio

You
- ◆ have an independence about you which enables you to live anywhere from a slum to a mansion.
- ◆ like a home with some individuality and one which reflects your unique personality.
- ◆ probably have a swimming pool or live near water.
- ◆ like to be permanent in your place of residence.

Sagittarius

You

◆ like a spacious home with facilities for outdoor living.

◆ aren't keen on housework as you find it so boring and repetitive.

◆ like all the modern household gadgets and labor-saving devices which your money can afford.

◆ can become irritable when you are restricted by home responsibilities.

Capricorn

You

◆ like your privacy from the neighbors and tend to worry about what people think.

◆ see to it that your home is clean and in good repair.

◆ dislike living in a noisy community and prefer your home to be set back from the street.

◆ prefer durable, conservative furniture and are not impressed by ultra-modern or cheap styles.

Aquarius

You
- ◆ think housework in general is a waste of time and are likely to seek quick methods of getting through it with maximum efficiency.
- ◆ like your home to be close to transport, shops and other conveniences.
- ◆ are a nature-lover and enjoy the beauty of a garden though you do not always spend the necessary time in it.
- ◆ dislike moving and like to remain settled in the one spot.

Pisces

You
- ◆ like a comfortable, spacious home.
- ◆ take good care of your home and like to keep it neat and tidy.
- ◆ like a restful home which is your place of refuge.
- ◆ are artistically tasteful in your choice of decor and your home is likely to have beautiful color coordination.

Family Affairs
• •

Aries

You
- ◆ have a youthful nature and enjoy children around you.
- ◆ are proud of your children and are a good companion to them.
- ◆ are usually a strict disciplinarian with your children and like to be respected.
- ◆ probably exert a strong influence in household matters.

Taurus

You
- ◆ are a family-orientated person.
- ◆ are usually patient but strict with your family.
- ◆ are a good provider to your family.
- ◆ generally keep family matters to yourself.

Gemini

You

- ◆ are not the ideal parent as you have difficulty being consistently firm with your children.
- ◆ may find that children sometimes upset your nervous system.
- ◆ are born under the sign which does not bear a lot of children.
- ◆ have a youthful streak in your nature and are understanding of your children's problems.

Cancer

You

- ◆ enjoy administering to the needs of your family.
- ◆ have a great respect and sense of responsibility towards your family and relations and your family tree.
- ◆ will probably have lots of comings, goings and changes in your family life.
- ◆ keenly see to it that your children are well provided for with the best that life can offer.

Leo

You

◆ should try to listen to both sides of any family argument.

◆ are inclined to worry too much about the upbringing of your children.

◆ manage household affairs with efficiency.

◆ like to feel your family needs you and respects you.

Virgo

You

◆ are devoted to your family's interests and comforts.

◆ would be wise to consider carefully your own nature and ambitions before planning to have a family.

◆ teach your children commonsense but you may be too demanding of them.

◆ believe that charity begins at home.

Libra

You
- are basically domestic by nature and enjoy having your own home.
- do not like solitude and enjoy having a family about you.
- are able to understand a child's point of view.
- are inclined to be too permissive, allowing your children to get their own way.

Scorpio

You
- take a great pride in your family.
- are ambitious for your children and would be wise not to drive them too hard.
- may neglect your family life if you are unhappy in your marriage.
- become disappointed if your children do not respond to your wishes and demands.

Sagittarius

You
- ◆ can adjust to being a homebody when the necessity arises.
- ◆ particularly enjoy your family when they mature and are developing their personalities.
- ◆ can communicate well with your children and can be a close companion to them.
- ◆ may have other interests which divert you from a wholly family-orientated existence.

Capricorn

You
- ◆ discipline your children and seldom pamper them.
- ◆ are prepared to undergo hardships for the sake of your children's education.
- ◆ like an orderly home life and keep to routines.
- ◆ sometimes put too much restraint on your children and they in turn can become resentful.

Aquarius

You

◆ make a good parent because of your gentle yet firm influence over your children.
◆ have the ability to encourage your children to grow as individual personalities.
◆ usually get on well with your children as you do not treat them as inferior beings.
◆ dislike being strongly bound by family ties and obligations but you are not irresponsible.

Pisces

You

◆ are loving, kind and considerate and bring these assets into your home.
◆ regard a happy family with great importance.
◆ tend to spoil your family and need to keep a firm upper hand.
◆ are prepared to make personal sacrifices for the sake of your children's welfare.

Making Friends

• •

Aries

You

◆ have the ability to make people feel at ease.

◆ are equally at ease in the company of kings or paupers.

◆ will meet a lot of people during the course of your life.

◆ are inclined to take people for what they appear to be and not for what they really are.

Taurus

You

◆ have a personality which attracts friends.

◆ dislike people who meddle in your personal affairs.

◆ like to keep company with people who are successful as you admire such people.

◆ make people feel at ease.

Gemini

You
- ◆ enjoy being in a crowd and mix well socially.
- ◆ can be quite selective in your choice of close friends.
- ◆ like to meet new people and exchange points of view.
- ◆ seldom move quickly into a close relationship.

Cancer

You
- ◆ have the ability to draw people towards you even though you sometimes hold yourself in reserve.
- ◆ are a person whom others take a long time to know well.
- ◆ will retreat into your shell when confronted with disagreeable or insensitive people.
- ◆ are not a bubbly, extroverted type of person and usually wait for other people to initiate a friendship.

Leo

You

◆ like to make many friends and are loyal and always available to those who need your help.

◆ have no trouble in making friends because of your outgoing, open personality.

◆ like to be seen in influential company.

◆ have a basic need to be liked and respected by the people you meet.

Virgo

You

◆ are discriminating in your choice of friends.

◆ like to associate with cultured, well-informed people.

◆ have a critical side to your nature as well as a natural reserve and these qualities may estrange you from friends.

◆ do not admire people who don't exert some effort.

Libra

You

◆ will make a large number of friends particularly through your social activities.
◆ will have little to do with the friendship of people who are indiscreet, untidy or irresponsible.
◆ try to understand each person as an individual.
◆ show consideration and appreciation of others and try to treat others as you would like to be treated.

Scorpio

You

◆ are not likely to make friends indiscriminately and can seemingly take or leave a friendship.
◆ are frequently accused of having an ulterior motive in your friendships but this is an unfair evaluation of you.
◆ constantly appear to be on the attack or defence about something.
◆ rarely make a neutral impression on people.

Sagittarius

You

◆ are forthright in your dealings with others and are able to inspire their immediate confidence.

◆ have an enthusiasm for life which is contagious to those about you.

◆ are likely to have a large social circle of friends.

◆ can be somewhat disagreeable, even hostile, with people you take a dislike to.

Capricorn

You

◆ do not attract a large number of friends.

◆ sometimes have difficulty choosing true friends and can be wary and reserved with people.

◆ gain people's respect by your reliability, dignity and courteous manner.

◆ need to get yourself out, to mingle with people and make an effort to be bright company.

Aquarius

You

◆ are able to get on well with all kinds of people because of your tolerant disposition.

◆ have a strong trust in people but this could lead you to many disappointments.

◆ should make friends because of your capacity to understand human nature.

◆ have a universal love for people but sometimes have difficulty making close personal relationships.

Pisces

You

◆ have a perception which instinctively tells you about people.

◆ benefit by the company of friends with a happy, outgoing attitude to life.

◆ seldom make bad friends and you rarely become involved in arguments.

◆ usually take people for what they are.

Being a Friend

• •

Aries

You

◆ are loyal to your friends and will aid them in difficult times.

◆ enjoy companionship and are happy when people drop in.

◆ will find people enjoy your wit and intellectual ability.

◆ have the ability to lead your own group.

Taurus

You

◆ have a soothing influence on people.

◆ enjoy entertaining and make a wonderful host.

◆ are a true friend in times of stress.

◆ stay a friend once you make a friend.

Gemini

You

◆ are generally sincere in your relationships.

◆ show consideration in return for others' kindness.

◆ can be changeable in your attitude towards people with whom you constantly associate.

◆ enjoy the company of friends and like to make others feel good.

Cancer

You

◆ respond with kindness and help when a friend in need turns to you.

◆ are more relaxed with tried and true friends and like to entertain your close friends at home.

◆ can ruin a friendship when you misinterpret an innocent remark.

◆ will be yourself with people you trust though you tend to radiate your moods to affect others.

Leo

You
- ◆ appreciate the respect you gain from a sincere friendship.
- ◆ are docile and pleasant in the company you enjoy.
- ◆ gain much happiness from having many friends about you.
- ◆ have the ability to give people a lift when they are feeling low.

Virgo

You
- ◆ like friends who have a particular direction in life and who win your admiration.
- ◆ are sometimes disappointed in your friendships as people seldom live up to your expectations.
- ◆ regard friends as security and can feel deserted without them.
- ◆ are always available for practical advice and happily lend a helping hand.

Libra

You
- ◆ are thoughtful of your friends especially at times of celebration.
- ◆ desire genuine friendship and are generous with those you like.
- ◆ expect your friends to reciprocate your generosity.
- ◆ enjoy having many friends and acquaintances and are keen to please everyone.

Scorpio

You
- ◆ need friends about you but you also need time on your own.
- ◆ need to keep in mind that friendship involves giving and taking, try not to become indignant over small matters.
- ◆ can't tolerate half-hearted attitudes, two-timers or goody-goodies amongst your friends.
- ◆ act according to your moods even when it comes to your need for companionship.

Sagittarius

You
◆ enjoy friends dropping in at any
   time to see you and you make sure
   that they are properly entertained.
◆ have a way about you which cheers
   up people and gives them a
   renewed courage and optimism.
◆ are not afraid to speak your mind
   clearly to your friends.
◆ tend to keep friends with similar
   interests and pursuits to your own.

Capricorn

You
◆ won't turn your back on others
   when they need you.
◆ do not like to be obligated to
   people and seldom ask for favors.
◆ would be wise to rid yourself of the
   habit of expecting others to prove
   their friendship to you.
◆ dislike visitors calling
   unexpectedly as you like to know
   and be organized in advance.

Aquarius

You

◆ probably won't have a large number of friends as your detached nature is not always easy to understand.
◆ can be a loyal and discreet friend, keeping many of your friends for life.
◆ may gather an odd collection of friends ranging from the timid to the eccentric.
◆ do not like your friends to display intensity or possessiveness.

Pisces

You

◆ are trusted as a friend and are often told deep secrets in confidence.
◆ like doing things for others and give freely to those you like and love.
◆ are understanding and sympathetic of others' problems.
◆ have a way about you which makes others feel comfortable in your company.

Leisure and You

Aries

You
- ◆ have a natural love of reading, music and the theatre.
- ◆ are good at sport and games and enjoy participation.
- ◆ are entertaining and good company and can thaw out the shyest person.
- ◆ enjoy the pleasures of travel and appreciate the beauties of nature.

Taurus

You
- ◆ enjoy music, singing and musical pursuits.
- ◆ have a flair for cooking and enjoy the pleasures of eating.
- ◆ are a creative gardener having "green thumbs".
- ◆ have a flair for artistic hobbies and these may be financially profitable.

Gemini

You
- ◆ have more diversified interests and talents than any other sign.
- ◆ like varied hobbies which may even be side-occupations.
- ◆ have a keen sense of appreciation particularly with regard to the arts and literature.
- ◆ frequently crusade for things you consider worthwhile for humanity.

Cancer

You
- ◆ are attracted to things with an emotional appeal.
- ◆ may excel as a public speaker in the organizations you join and can run fundraising campaigns efficiently.
- ◆ enjoy different topics of study and you have the ability to learn almost anything when you put your mind to it.
- ◆ like to make collections of old things and you have an affinity with antiques and old homes.

Leo

You
- ◆ seldom have a solitary hobby as you prefer to mix with people.
- ◆ enjoy any leisure-time pursuit in which you can express yourself.
- ◆ have a tremendous drive and enthusiasm for leisure-time pursuits.
- ◆ like having a busy social life and can capably mix business with pleasure.

Virgo

You
- ◆ are a good host and this impresses your friends.
- ◆ have an active mind and enjoy learning about your environment and human relations.
- ◆ are handy about the house and often prefer to do things yourself to save money.
- ◆ enjoy humor about realistic happenings and like to engage in witty, subtle conversation.

Libra

You

- ◆ have a love of all things beautiful and this is reflected in your taste for good music, furniture, paintings, wines and the like.
- ◆ probably have cultural interests and pursue these in your leisure time.
- ◆ are a good sport and know how to display team spirit.
- ◆ like intellectual humor but are not keen on slapstick comedy.

Scorpio

You

- ◆ enjoy becoming involved in games which involve skill or chance.
- ◆ like competition in sport as you like to win.
- ◆ are often known for the good things you achieve in the community.
- ◆ benefit from your ability to appreciate beauty in its many forms.

Sagittarius

You
- ◆ take an interest in public affairs and could join the executive of an organization.
- ◆ have a great capacity for enjoying life and you know how to gain some gratification from each of your pursuits.
- ◆ are constantly on the go and it appears that physical activity is a must for your well-being.
- ◆ enjoy discussing progressive ideas and presenting your points of view.

Capricorn

You
- ◆ probably become absorbed in one leisure activity at a time.
- ◆ like to study anything which will help you get ahead.
- ◆ may try your hand at home improvements but remember to treat this as a leisure activity, not as work.
- ◆ may enjoy a hobby in which you make a collection of things such as stamps, coins or recipes.

129

Aquarius

You

◆ have an in-built need to associate yourself with a worthwhile cause.
◆ are likely to take on an extra course of study in a subject which captures your interest.
◆ are usually busy doing something and have a great need to experience all that life has to offer.
◆ are interested in cultural life including theatre, music, art, ballet and lectures.

Pisces

You

◆ show aptitudes in the world of the arts, such as music, painting and poetry, for in these you can forget the hard realities of life.
◆ may find completeness and overcome any emotional instability through some philosophical or psychic study.
◆ respond to music and are probably good at dancing.
◆ have genuine love and affection for animals.

Recreational Activities

●●●●●●●●●●●●●●●●●●●●●●●●●●●●●●●●

Aries

You

◆ need an interest which will relax your mind and nerves.
◆ would be wise to have regular exercise and engage in a sport which you enjoy.
◆ need to be with people where you can express your views.
◆ enjoy meeting new and interesting people.

Taurus

You

◆ like giving parties but are not frivolous about it.
◆ enjoy a vacation at home as you are not comfortable in unfamiliar surroundings.
◆ enjoy outdoor entertainment such as picnics, barbecues and social games.
◆ find music has a harmonious influence on you.

Gemini

You

♦ are fond of traveling and seeing different places.

♦ require frequent recreational breaks from your normal surroundings whenever possible, to appease your restlessness.

♦ probably have a practical handiwork pursuit as your hobby.

♦ are a person who always likes to be busy even in recreational time.

Cancer

You

♦ like to take your holidays near the sea as you enjoy water pursuits.

♦ enjoy travel as it satisfies your curiosity but you are equally glad to return home.

♦ will probably spend much of your leisure time entertaining or relaxing at home.

♦ may spend some of your recreation time doing humanitarian work and may be inclined towards religious pursuits.

Leo

You
- ◆ like active rather than passive forms of relaxation.
- ◆ are fond of theatre, parties, music, races, fairs, sports, pageants and many forms of entertainment.
- ◆ are generous in your interests which will often involve you in organizations and clubs.
- ◆ rarely need the solitude that is so necessary for most other signs.

Virgo

You
- ◆ like to travel but prefer to stay away from the crowds.
- ◆ enjoy a variety of interests as a result of your curiosity and particularly like cultural pursuits.
- ◆ like quiet, unhurried holidays preferably in a natural setting.
- ◆ love over-sleeping but may enjoy work as a form of recreation for you don't like wasting time.

Libra

You
- ◆ probably like being involved in club work and may take on an executive position.
- ◆ like to be surrounded by congenial people on your holidays and you make a pleasant vacation partner.
- ◆ like hobbies in which beauty prevails, such as collections of lovely things.
- ◆ love parties and social gatherings and you enjoy dressing up for the occasion.

Scorpio

You
- ◆ like to indulge in luxuries when you are financial.
- ◆ need time to quietly withdraw and during these moments you may enjoy listening to music, reading or other quiet activities.
- ◆ tend to be attracted to religious or occult interests.
- ◆ probably like camping and setting off on the unbeaten track for you can easily deny yourself the comforts of modern living.

Sagittarius

You
- ◆ like to lead an active out-of-doors life.
- ◆ like to keep in touch with current affairs and often engage in recreational reading and studying.
- ◆ will probably travel and enjoy various changes throughout your life.
- ◆ show a fondness for music, art, poetry, sports, games and the theatre.

Capricorn

You
- ◆ should take a holiday or try a hobby which provides you with a change of pace and scene.
- ◆ enjoy organised recreational activities amongst friends, such as bowling, golf, card games and entertaining on a small scale.
- ◆ prefer a vacation at an established, respectable resort.
- ◆ like to visit places of historical interest and see things which are steeped in tradition.

Aquarius

You
- ◆ like recreational activities of a social nature.
- ◆ are attracted to the strange, the different, the unconventional, the "way out" and the extraordinary.
- ◆ like sports but will probably avoid the more strenuous games.
- ◆ enjoy travelling and will probably travel extensively during your lifetime.

Pisces

You
- ◆ are fond of the sea and water pursuits such as swimming, fishing and boating.
- ◆ may seek an artistic interest as it is a means of expressing your feelings and escaping daily routines and pressures.
- ◆ enjoy travel and the occasional change of scene seems essential to your well-being.
- ◆ need time to be alone to dream and to recuperate from the rush of everyday life.

Health Indications

Aries

You

◆ have great spurts of energy followed by physical exhaustion.
◆ do not like being ill although you usually recover from illness quickly.
◆ seldom get through life without experiencing the surgeon's knife.
◆ can't stand physical pain and can be cowardly about anything that hurts.

Taurus

You

◆ generally have a strong, robust constitution.
◆ are inclined to drink and eat to excess.
◆ bear up well and have little complaint when ill but are slow to recover from sickness.
◆ can withstand great physical and mental stress and rarely become fatigued.

137

Gemini

You
- ◆ do not make a good patient as you are inclined to ignore medical advice and can be neglectful of ailments.
- ◆ rarely suffer from obesity as a result of your high-speed physical and mental drive.
- ◆ have a good physical resilience; however, your inability to relax may prove harmful.
- ◆ often try to accomplish too much and may quickly tire yourself out.

Cancer

You
- ◆ were born under a sign which indicates a long life span.
- ◆ have a fear of pain and illness.
- ◆ do not have great recuperative powers.
- ◆ can play on sympathy if you are not well and don't always make a good patient.

Leo

You

♦ are a robust person who radiates great vitality.
♦ generally have a strong resistance to disease and recuperate quickly from an illness.
♦ can be careless about your health at times but dislike being ill and confined to bed.
♦ generally expend a lot of energy and this may lead to nervous strain.

Virgo

You

♦ usually retain your youthful looks more than any other sign.
♦ become nervous and upset if life does not run as smoothly as your orderly nature desires.
♦ probably have a medicine cupboard which is very well stocked.
♦ are a sensible patient and like a doctor to take time to explain the treatment to you.

Libra

You
◆ appear healthy to others because of your grooming and personal care.
◆ like to be given lots of attention and sympathy when you are ill.
◆ have a natural vitality but often become tired because of social obligations.
◆ often outlive others because of your moderate living and natural good judgment.

Scorpio

You
◆ have a strong constitution together with good resistance to illness.
◆ benefit from outdoor activities which enable you to release any built-in tensions.
◆ have the courage to endure pain and have excellent recuperative powers.
◆ probably dislike going to doctors, taking medicine or going to bed when ill.

Sagittarius

You

- ◆ generally appear to be quite athletic, healthy and physically fit.
- ◆ are inclined to ignore any symptoms of ill-health which can cause you a later setback.
- ◆ are more accident-prone than most people because of your impatience and restlessness.
- ◆ have a youthful appearance later in life because of your cheerful optimism and variety of interests.

Capricorn

You

- ◆ are aware of the benefits of moderation and good sense where your health is concerned.
- ◆ could age quickly as a result of constant worrying.
- ◆ usually take the necessary steps to remedy any ailments.
- ◆ have good endurance and an instinct for your own survival and self-preservation.

141

Aquarius

You
- ◆ generally have a strong resistance to illness.
- ◆ may have health problems if someone is dominating you or having a bad influence on you.
- ◆ will find that worry and pressure are more likely to cause you illness than anything else.
- ◆ generally have good recuperative powers, especially if you can enjoy quiet, restful times and be at one with nature.

Pisces

You
- ◆ often look younger than you really are and generally live to a grand old age if you do not abuse your body.
- ◆ have a fairly slow metabolism and may turn to drink or drugs to give you a lift.
- ◆ can be upset by changes.
- ◆ may give the impression that you have delicate health but you generally have a strong constitution.

Keeping Good Health

Aries

◆ Avoid overworking and recognize when to stop and rest.
◆ Learn to relax and not to be so headstrong, and practice moderation in all things.
◆ Take more notice of symptoms and see your doctor and dentist for regular checkups.
◆ Take care in activities which have an element of risk and particularly protect your head and face.

Taurus

◆ Keep active as laziness is detrimental to your health.
◆ Avoid damp places and wet climates.
◆ Watch the waistline as a result of self-indulgence.
◆ Take particular care of your throat and act promptly when ailments appear.

Gemini

- ◆ Seek a calm environment to avoid upsetting your nervous system.
- ◆ Slow down and avoid being constantly on the go.
- ◆ Have a substantial amount of sleep.
- ◆ Practice deep breathing and chest exercise or do a little walking and get regular doses of fresh air.

Cancer

- ◆ Organize your life along simple, regulated routines.
- ◆ Avoid tense situations and becoming upset over little things.
- ◆ Stay away from excitement or strain as it usually affects your digestion or nervous system.
- ◆ Avoid gulping down your food and try to remain quiet after a meal.

Leo

◆ Be less intense about things.
◆ Take care not to overwork yourself into physical, mental or nervous exhaustion.
◆ Have scheduled periods of rest and relaxation to conserve a little bit of your energy.
◆ Eat, drink and be merry in moderation as you are inclined to indulge in excesses.

Virgo

◆ Seek peace and harmony in your home and work environment.
◆ Eat in a calm atmosphere and avoid hard-to-digest foods as well as alcohol.
◆ Avoid doing too much as you can drive yourself to ill-health.
◆ Take time to relax and enjoy the sunlight and fresh air.

Libra

◆ Follow a light diet and get plenty of fresh air.
◆ Seek peace and harmony in your surroundings.
◆ Avoid crowds as you are inclined to claustrophobia.
◆ Seek an environment away from any form of ugliness as this can make you physically and emotionally ill.

Scorpio

◆ Curb your tendency to overeat and over-drink.
◆ Seek medical advice when initial symptoms appear.
◆ Stop worrying and overdoing things as this will make you old before your time.
◆ Try doing things with less intensity and use moderation in your approach to sex.

Sagittarius

◆ Seek moderation in all things.
◆ Be more cautious with your appetite and avoid being overindulgent.
◆ Avoid physical risks whereby you may be injured.
◆ Avoid excessive worry for this will cause a loss of vitality.

Capricorn

◆ Approach each day with renewed interest and optimism.
◆ Become more casual and easy-going with yourself as this will make life happier for you and those around you.
◆ Avoid bottling up your worries and give them some release.
◆ Drink non-alcoholic liquids and eat easily digested foods.

Aquarius

◆ Train yourself to keep control of your mind and don't let your worries get the better of your health.

◆ Avoid circumstances in which you give too much energy and tire yourself out quickly.

◆ Seek peace, quiet and harmony in your surroundings.

◆ Guard against carelessness with your diet and any excesses.

Pisces

◆ Have harmonious surroundings for your physical as well as mental comfort.

◆ Avoid bad weather, especially overexposure to cold and dampness.

◆ Control negative and over-imaginative thoughts.

◆ Remember that your good health is in your own hands and that no one forces you into bad habits.

The Female Sunsign
. . . .

Aries

You
- are a youthful and witty person, with a wide range of interests and general knowledge.
- have a great deal of charm, optimism and are a good sport.
- can be temperamental and become icy when hurt.
- have an outward confidence but an inward vulnerability.

Taurus

You
- have a beauty and charm about you that is difficult to define.
- are a practical rather than idealistic person.
- can be domineering in your own quiet way.
- have a naturally happy disposition and are level-headed.

149

Gemini

You

◆ generally have a fun-loving disposition.
◆ are thoughtful of the comfort of others.
◆ need variety in your life and like to make new friends.
◆ baffle people with your changing ways and moods.

Cancer

You

◆ are generally loving and outgoing with a happy disposition.
◆ have changeable moods which can bewilder others.
◆ like to dress well.
◆ probably have an artistic talent and enjoy intellectual pursuits.

Leo

You

◆ radiate a warmth wherever you go and are usually liked and respected.
◆ have the ability to succeed in any work which takes your interest.
◆ enjoy the luxuries of life and for this reason, money is important to you.
◆ enjoy an active social life, especially parties and entertainment.

Virgo

You

◆ are aware of your own imperfections and worry about them.
◆ love deeply but usually express your love in practical ways.
◆ are a neat and tidy person both in your appearance and your home.
◆ are a warm-hearted, kind person with a sense of responsibility.

Libra

You
- are feminine, graceful and gentle but can take charge when necessary.
- enjoy conversing and listening to the opinions of others.
- have a great need for harmony and may even weaken your principles to compromise.
- like to be well-dressed and like fine quality in the things around you.

Scorpio

You
- have a realistic outlook on life and are prepared to accept people as they are.
- have a determined, persevering approach to life.
- are intuitive, perceptive and have a highly developed sixth sense.
- become moody or overbearing when you are dissatisfied with your lot.

Sagittarius

You
◆ have a restless, high-spirited nature and the fortitude to be able to hide your heartaches.
◆ are an outdoors type, enjoying social and sporting activities.
◆ have a happy, easy-going disposition but can be too outspoken.
◆ are independent and broad-minded and regard males as your equals.

Capricorn

You
◆ have high ideals and devote yourself to them wholeheartedly.
◆ are efficient and have many capabilities which are admired by people who know you.
◆ sometimes appear aloof and can conceal your true feelings with detached reserve.
◆ are basically kind-hearted, patient, sensitive and endeavor to uphold justice.

Aquarius

You

◆ are capable, adaptable and probably a talented person.
◆ don't like being tied down as you need your freedom and individuality.
◆ can be unpredictable and have your own code of ethics.
◆ enjoy a social life, have a wide range of interests and can adapt to all social situations.

Pisces

You

◆ are untiring in your efforts to accomplish your aims.
◆ are sentimental and dream about the ideal romance.
◆ have a certain mystique and charm about you.
◆ sometimes think you are inadequate and have doubts about yourself and so become depressed.

Women and Their Partners

●●●●●●●●●●●●●●●●●●●●●●●●●●●●●●●●

Aries

You

◆ are a thoughtful and considerate companion and enjoy a social life with male company.
◆ are easily inspired by a loyal and devoted partner.
◆ have plenty of affection to give the right partner.
◆ like a partner who has a degree of domination over you.

Taurus

You

◆ regard marriage as a serious business and are capable of taking the good with the bad.
◆ give your partner the support he needs in his career.
◆ are determined to make your relationship work.
◆ can be possessive and demanding of your partner's complete attention.

Gemini

You

◆ have little trouble attracting members of the opposite sex.
◆ like to be regarded as an equal.
◆ enjoy a relationship with a partner who is not intellectually inferior.
◆ need a partner who is tolerant enough to stand by you while you are indulging your moods.

Cancer

You

◆ give your heart to the one you love and will remain loyal as long as you are emotionally secure.
◆ should be careful not to put your husband into second place when your family arrives.
◆ respect a man who is protective of you and gives you reassurance of his love.
◆ are willing to make sacrifices in order to make your relationship work.

Leo

You

◆ enjoy a partnership with a lively personality and satisfying lover.

◆ want to be a loyal, responsible partner.

◆ enjoy receiving attention from your partner and actually believe you are entitled to it.

◆ are serious in your romantic attachments but usually confine your display of affection to moments of privacy.

Virgo

You

◆ have a serious view of marriage and believe in doing everything possible to make it work.

◆ may need to be a little more tolerant of your partner's shortcomings.

◆ are as ambitious for your partner as you are for yourself.

◆ are an independent person and may actually benefit by staying single.

Libra

You

◆ make a fine companion for your partner and are responsive to his needs.

◆ seem to possess a mysterious charm which attracts the opposite sex.

◆ are genuinely interested in your partner's activities because teamwork is important to you.

◆ love to be loved and adored and enjoy having things done for you by your mate.

Scorpio

You

◆ will be a devoted partner providing you make a success of your love life and get enough affection.

◆ support your husband in his career and interests and will stand up for him if necessary.

◆ won't excuse weakness in a man and need to respect the man in your life.

◆ answer to no law but your own; it is you who will decide if you want to make a success of your relationship.

Sagittarius

You

◆ are faithful in marriage and expect your relationship to be lasting.
◆ like to share business interests with your partner and talk over problems and opinions with him.
◆ prefer to be more of a companion than a lover in your relationship.
◆ live life to the full with your partner.

Capricorn

You

◆ would be wise not to organize your partner too much in his habits and work routines.
◆ can be unhappy in married life if you do not find an outlet for your abilities.
◆ are careful with your affections and not openly romantic.
◆ have a strong need for material and monetary security and therefore need a partner who is reliable.

Aquarius

You

◆ can be emotionally responsive though you are ruled by your intellect.

◆ like to share in the work and success of your partner.

◆ still value your freedom and individuality after marriage, as well as your privacy.

◆ would change your partner without regret if you felt the change was justified.

Pisces

You

◆ need a dependable partner who can help you make decisions.

◆ need to show some patience to give your marriage every chance of success.

◆ can be among the most loving and devoted of wives.

◆ want to care for and protect your partner and seldom want to dominate him.

Women at Home

Aries

You
- ◆ expend boundless energy on your home and family.
- ◆ are capable of coping on a household budget when necessary.
- ◆ are a quick, efficient home-manager, but may also make a success of a career.
- ◆ make your home a comfortable place but you also need to make an effort to provide a calm atmosphere.

Taurus

You
- ◆ like keeping your home neat and comfortable.
- ◆ are a devoted mother and partner.
- ◆ have a deep understanding and sympathy for those you love.
- ◆ find the most satisfaction in life from your home and family.

Gemini

You

◆ like a comfortable, attractive home to reflect your personality.
◆ are the radiant center of love for your family.
◆ like to add your imaginative touch to furnishing and decor.
◆ can easily become dissatisfied with the sameness of housekeeping.

Cancer

You

◆ run a neat, tidy and orderly home and endeavor to make it a harmonious one.
◆ take the role of motherhood seriously and make the best of mothers.
◆ treasure your possessions in the home.
◆ are more inclined to be at ease in the home than in the business world.

Leo

You

◆ expect respect and obedience from your family.

◆ like to entertain and have a flair for cooking.

◆ enjoy your share of socializing as well as attending to domestic duties.

◆ do all you can to see to it that your children are brought up correctly.

Virgo

You

◆ may be a strict mother with your children but you only have their interests at heart.

◆ enjoy looking after the people you love and also enjoy the security your home provides.

◆ like to rearrange things about your home, using your keen sense of beauty and harmony.

◆ are efficient in household management and careful with the budget.

Libra

You

- ◆ have expensive tastes and must make an effort to keep within the family budget.
- ◆ have a talent of bringing happiness and peace into your home.
- ◆ like a varied social life but never neglect your family or home duties.
- ◆ need a creative activity outside the home, as you may become depressed if housebound.

Scorpio

You

- ◆ have a home which in some way reflects your individual touch.
- ◆ probably have many family battles but these are usually confined to the home.
- ◆ do what you can to bring up your children correctly and teach them to meet life's difficulties.
- ◆ may be lacking in tenderness and in openly displaying affection to your children.

Sagittarius

You
- ◆ do all your housework well but don't spend all your time on domestic chores.
- ◆ are cheerful and among the best of mothers.
- ◆ always like to keep busy and have little patience with those who waste their time.
- ◆ can make a success of a career as well as of your home duties.

Capricorn

You
- ◆ manage the household with efficiency and make your home a comfortable place.
- ◆ should avoid being overbearing and domineering with your family.
- ◆ keep up-to-date with your household duties.
- ◆ spend money wisely.

Aquarius

You

◆ don't like anything to upset the peace and harmony in your home.
◆ set a good example to your children and are a devoted mother.
◆ are not very domestically inclined.
◆ like to have the latest time-saving appliances.

Pisces

You

◆ do not spare yourself in the service of your family.
◆ are probably too soft and impatient in the discipline of your children.
◆ have an eye for detail and like your housework done systematically and carefully.
◆ are happiest when doing things for your family and friends.

The Male Sunsign

Aries

You

◆ are self-assured and are bursting with ideas and creative energy.

◆ quickly lose your optimism when you lose your authority.

◆ can at times be exasperatingly thoughtless, selfish, demanding, impatient and intolerant and you hate to admit you are wrong.

◆ are a friendly, independent person who enjoys living life to the fullest.

Taurus

You

◆ are generally practical and hardworking.

◆ can be stubborn and gruff and refuse to give in when annoyed.

◆ have a quiet exterior which may hide a passionate nature.

◆ are slow and methodical but have unusual physical strength and endurance.

Gemini

You

◆ have an adventurous nature and a restlessness which may puzzle those around you.
◆ may change friendships on a whim.
◆ have fussy standards and can be critical when things don't appear proper in your eyes.
◆ are inclined to leave work unfinished.

Cancer

You

◆ have a natural reserve which women find hard to understand.
◆ love to be well cared for, given lots of attention and well fed.
◆ can be moody, crabby and pessimistic.
◆ possess a sharp perception and keen intuition.

Leo

You

◆ have an independent nature like the lion and prefer to rule rather than be ruled.

◆ have the courage to charge ahead in the face of all opposition and a temper to be respected when aroused.

◆ like to get your own way using your dominant, forceful personality.

◆ have a personality which attracts people and therefore you can achieve great popularity.

Virgo

You

◆ are a practical person and appreciate the value of money.

◆ were born with an instinctive love of work.

◆ have mostly conventional, even conservative ideas.

◆ seek quality and dislike sloppiness and ignorance.

Libra

You
- ◆ have an intense love of excitement and you have a persuasive charm about you.
- ◆ frequently change your mind and can be indecisive and inconsistent.
- ◆ are extroverted and often talkative.
- ◆ have a habit of rationalizing things.

Scorpio

You
- ◆ lean towards excesses in drink, drugs, food and sex.
- ◆ are inclined to be dogmatic and can be demanding of those around you.
- ◆ can be moody and are inclined to brood by yourself.
- ◆ can bluff others with your cool exterior but actually boil with emotion underneath.

Sagittarius

You
◆ are a semi-reliant person and quickly take advantage of any opportunities available.
◆ can be impatient, dislike restraint and hate being delayed as you like to be prompt.
◆ are a good conversationalist and show an interest in a wide selection of topics.
◆ are the supreme optimist but can be easily misled and often form biased opinions.

Capricorn

You
◆ are not afraid of hard work and quickly grasp at opportunities.
◆ like to function to routines and schedules.
◆ are basically steady, dependable and serious and have a dry sense of humor.
◆ can be too cautious, suspicious and exacting and lacking in a sense of fun.

171

Aquarius

You
- ◆ have complex reactions to different situations which make it hard for others to really get to know you.
- ◆ possess a kind and generous nature and have a humanitarian outlook.
- ◆ sometimes avoid things you dislike rather than face them.
- ◆ are an independent person and seldom reveal your true feelings.

Pisces

You
- ◆ are generally easy to get along with, though you often procrastinate.
- ◆ have a tendency to be careless of your personal welfare.
- ◆ have a tender nature, are easily hurt and often feel lonely.
- ◆ may be intellectually brilliant and truthful, or, conversely, lazy and unreliable.

Men and Their Partners

●●●●●●●●●●●●●●●●●●●●●●●●●●●●●●●●

Aries

You

◆ tend to be a flirt, but become annoyed if your partner behaves the same way.

◆ are probably a virile person, having a good physique and a demanding sexual appetite.

◆ are usually a reliable and responsible mate once married, especially if you have made a wise choice.

◆ must remember that marriage is a partnership.

Taurus

You

◆ look for a partner who is a good homemaker.

◆ expect complete loyalty and devotion from your partner.

◆ are faithful and kind once married and enjoy making your partner happy.

◆ sometimes ignore your partner's plea to go out.

Gemini

You
- need a partner who is understanding and patient.
- can be ardent or placid depending on your mood and circumstances.
- desire a true and lasting love relationship.
- are generally a loving, responsible partner once you have found the person you are looking for.

Cancer

You
- enjoy female attention and like to be mothered to some extent.
- could be restless and insecure without the love and understanding of a partner.
- sometimes hide your true feelings for fear of being hurt or rejected.
- take married life seriously and like to settle down into your own home.

Leo

You
- ◆ like to feel your partner is dependent on you.
- ◆ need a partner who has a modifying effect on you as you are inclined to blow problems out of proportion.
- ◆ tend to organise your partner's affairs and expect unquestionable faithfulness.
- ◆ are likely to be faithful, though women are attracted to your charming ways.

Virgo

You
- ◆ are generally good-natured, kind and pleasant to be with.
- ◆ aren't inclined to dominate in a partnership.
- ◆ may prefer to be a bachelor; this is common for Virgos.
- ◆ do not always feel passionate but can be a flirt when the opportunity presents itself.

Libra

You
- ◆ need to be given lots of affection from your partner and loathe unfaithfulness.
- ◆ may have difficulty maintaining a faithful long-term relationship.
- ◆ can be somewhat demanding of your partner as you have many needs to be satisfied.
- ◆ may lack a true understanding of your partner's needs.

Scorpio

You
- ◆ you have a great influence over your partner and should choose someone who is willing to give in to your wishes.
- ◆ will probably have a marriage full of ups and downs.
- ◆ need to keep your jealous streak under control or your marriage will be a lost cause.
- ◆ seldom give yourself completely in a relationship but, rather, keep a little of yourself in reserve.

Sagittarius

You

◆ devote most of your energy to life in general and may hold little in reserve for your personal life.

◆ need to overlook your partner's faults and remember that no one is perfect.

◆ should look for a partner who is a good sport and has a sense of fun if she is to understand you.

◆ can be impulsive in your expressions of love; physical love is important to you.

Capricorn

You

◆ are happiest when mated with a thrifty person who agrees with your philosophy to save for a rainy day.

◆ often express your love in practical and material ways.

◆ should guard against becoming possessive and jealous of your partner.

◆ can make a faithful, loyal and protective partner.

Aquarius

You

◆ are not a passionate person but more of a companion.

◆ do not dictate do's and don't's to your partner as you believe she should express her own free will.

◆ seek a wife who is constant and consistent rather than glamorous.

◆ will be happiest when married to an intellectual woman with an interest in the humanities similar to yours.

Pisces

You

◆ need a partner who is more positive and realistic in outlook than yourself.

◆ require a partner who understands your moods and dreams.

◆ can be everything your partner wants you to be or sometimes completely the reverse.

◆ have a vast capacity for love and can be amongst the most generous and considerate of husbands.

Men at Home
· ·

Aries

You
◆ consider yourself in charge of your household.
◆ like to feel proud of your children but will be disappointed in them if they do not live up to your standards.
◆ are a family man, although you should belong to an organization where you can express your opinions.
◆ appreciate the comforts your home can provide, but also like to travel and enjoy adventurous pursuits.

Taurus

You
◆ rarely neglect your home for outside interests.
◆ are a strict father, believing this is for your child's own good.
◆ are hardworking and strive to provide the material needs of your family.
◆ try to boss your family around.

Gemini

You
- ◆ should guard against being too strict and inconsistent with your children.
- ◆ are not entirely home-orientated although you do derive pleasure from having a partner, family and home of your own.
- ◆ enjoy the challenge of raising children; they hold a fascination for you.
- ◆ dislike monotony and look for diversions when life becomes boring at home.

Cancer

You
- ◆ hold your children's success as a high priority.
- ◆ like to spend time with your family around the home.
- ◆ try to uphold family traditions with your children.
- ◆ regard your home as your castle.

Leo

You

◆ like to feel proud of your family and are particularly pleased when given favorable comments about them.
◆ are inclined to be too strict and authoritarian with your children.
◆ like to be the one to run things in the home.
◆ make a good repairer about the home.

Virgo

You

◆ work hard at giving your family a good life.
◆ don't usually yearn for fatherhood but will be a responsible parent.
◆ enjoy working about the home and seeing to it that things are functioning efficiently.
◆ detest disharmony in the home.

Libra

You

◆ like stability in your home and do what you can to keep things orderly.

◆ have a quiet authority and make a good husband and father when settled.

◆ have a sense of fairness with your children.

◆ are generally careful with the home budget.

◆ Encourage other family members to express their desires.

Scorpio

You

◆ work hard to get ahead as a family.

◆ expect respect for your role in the home.

◆ can be stubborn and selfish in decisions pertaining to home life.

◆ make it difficult to have harmony in the home as you dominate the scene.

Sagittarius

You

◆ are not a home-loving person but manage your household affairs capably when necessary.

◆ should avoid dominating your children and bragging about them to others.

◆ develop strong ties with your children when you figure out their individual personalities.

◆ are not particularly domesticated; your interests usually lie in your career or social pursuits.

Capricorn

You

◆ should avoid dominating the family and restricting your partner's authority.

◆ are not always understood by your children who may undervalue you.

◆ won't spare the rod and you can take your responsibility as father too seriously.

◆ can be miserly with money.

Aquarius

You

◆ are frequently absent from home as a result of your outside interests and you do not try to run the household.

◆ usually do things about the house when it suits you.

◆ are loved by children because you don't talk down to them.

◆ treat your family with consideration and you are able to inspire cooperation and harmony in the home.

Pisces

You

◆ are loved by your children for you listen to their problems.

◆ appreciate the finer things in life and do your best to bring them into your home.

◆ are hardworking and try to make your home secure and comfortable.

◆ need to be alone sometimes in order to untangle yourself from everyday problems.

Sunsigns and Babies

Aries

The Arian baby
◆ will be demanding of your time and patience and needs to be kept busy.
◆ can be quick-tempered and have sudden tantrums for no apparent reason.
◆ will probably walk and talk early and will be quick to show likes and dislikes in food.
◆ becomes grumpy when overtired and needs a lot of sleep to recover from highly active waking hours.

Taurus

The Taurean baby
◆ is generally a quiet baby but needs constant affection.
◆ needs a sense of permanency and may be unsettled in strange surroundings.
◆ is gentle-natured and cheerful most of the time but can be extremely stubborn.
◆ should have a good appetite and will happily settle down with music or TV.

Gemini

The Gemini baby
- has a happy, cheerful nature and likes to be the center of attention.
- will probably talk early and acquire a substantial vocabulary.
- will be inquisitive about anything and everything.
- is changeable from one day to the next, seldom reacting the same way.

Cancer

The Cancerian baby
- needs to be kept in close contact with its parents at first and needs a lot of cuddles to make it feel wanted.
- likes to be at home; becomes very attached to its parents and may not adjust well to staying at other people's homes.
- will enjoy things that appeal to the senses and playing games with imaginary characters.
- should not be forced to eat when upset because of a weak digestion and is best suited to several small meals a day.

Leo

The Leo baby
- likes to be the center of attention and is upset by indifference.
- can have emotional outbursts which are really release valves for stifled energy.
- doesn't like being kept in confined surroundings and has a boundless urge to keep moving.
- enjoys playing noisy games with other children and delights in big parties.

Virgo

The Virgo baby
- has a generous nature and is generally a pleasant infant.
- can be selective about food and may get indigestion and sometimes be constipated.
- likes creative toys and puzzles and will be tidy and careful with these.
- seems to have adult attitudes at an early age and is generally an undemanding child.

Libra

The Libran baby
◆ shouldn't be rushed and needs gentle but firm handling from an early age.
◆ is happiest in quiet, congenial surroundings and can be upset by violence or sudden noise.
◆ should be given one thing at a time as choices will only be confusing.
◆ needs lots of encouragement to overcome a lack of confidence.

Scorpio

The Scorpian baby
◆ is generally strong and healthy and has a quick recovery from illness.
◆ is a bundle of energy and seems to have an inbuilt, overcharged battery.
◆ wants to get its own way and is very determined and therefore needs patient parents who are willing to give a little.
◆ will take notice of what you do and learns quickly.

Sagittarius

The Sagittarian baby
- ◆ is generally a happy and friendly baby but will try your patience on many occasions.
- ◆ shows an early enthusiasm for life and will be constantly on the go.
- ◆ will be alert to all that is going on around it and likes an audience for its pranks.
- ◆ ensures your life is never dull and will need your constant attention.

Capricorn

The Capricornian baby
- ◆ seems to be independent from an early age and will show a strong will.
- ◆ is prone to childhood illnesses and common ailments.
- ◆ is never shy about making its needs and wishes known.
- ◆ needs demonstrative affection more than most children and can wear you down until you give in.

189

Aquarius

The Aquarian baby
- ◆ will often appear preoccupied with its own thoughts and show early signs of independence and determination.
- ◆ can show changes of attitude, mood and interests from day to day.
- ◆ should not be loudly scolded when in error but spoken to quietly and sensibly and praised whenever possible.
- ◆ can be left to play happily by itself and also gets on well with other children.

Pisces

The Piscean baby
- ◆ has charming, irresistible ways which may weaken your use of discipline.
- ◆ may have erratic, fussy sleeping and feeding habits and will seldom fit into a daily routine. (Try using a make-believe character while feeding.)
- ◆ will be a little actor from the beginning but doesn't like rough play or "horsing" around.
- ◆ identifies quickly with people and reacts to them at once.

The Growing Years

• •

Aries

Arian children

◆ will be independent but still require a lot of affection and guidance.

◆ are naturally honest and should be trusted with responsibility.

◆ should be asked rather than given orders which will probably be defied.

◆ are usually good at sports and will probably enjoy music, theatrics and other artistic forms.

Taurus

Taurean children

◆ have a slow but retentive mind and orderly habits.

◆ normally have a calm, cheerful and pleasant disposition.

◆ will be conscientious students and will work best without being pushed.

◆ do not like being unfairly treated and can build up a lasting resentment.

Gemini

Gemini children

◆ dislike being hemmed in by unrelenting routines or boring work.
◆ are quick, versatile and impatient but not deliberately callous.
◆ appreciate the freedom to make their own decisions.
◆ are likely to be successful at doing two things at once, such as doing homework and watching TV.

Cancer

Cancerian children

◆ are not always forthright in speech or action and require positive encouragement and motivation.
◆ need to be taught to stand on their own two feet away from home.
◆ can become sullen and feel hurt and neglected if they do not get the attention they seek.
◆ are often over-sensitive emotionally and need helpful reassurance and gentle discipline.

Leo

Leo children
◆ are popular with other children and are born with a natural ability for leadership.
◆ generally enjoy life and are happiest when busy.
◆ need to be given some freedom and also their own spending money.
◆ will tend to reject authority; are best disciplined by ignoring their demands and using indirect motivation rather than direct orders.

Virgo

Virgo children
◆ try hard to please and should require very little reprimand.
◆ are quick to form likes and dislikes and can criticize with amusing accuracy.
◆ need a room of their own for they like their privacy.
◆ probably have a musical or artistic ability which should be encouraged.

193

Libra

Libran children

◆ have a keen intuition and peaceful disposition which could be destroyed by nagging and too much parental supervision.

◆ quickly take on attitudes of people with whom they associate.

◆ are easy to get along with and will probably have many friends.

◆ enjoy group activities, team sports and show a liking for music.

Scorpio

Scorpian children

◆ have a natural shyness which they cover up with a bold and apparently self-confident exterior.

◆ need to learn to consider others, to be tolerant, and to be good sports.

◆ will not always do as they are told and may go out of their way to be disobedient.

◆ need to have their energy channelled into something constructive and challenging.

Sagittarius

Sagittarian children
◆ love to have lots of friends about and will be off after school to play with others.
◆ are frank and honest when expressing their opinions but can be rude and hot-headed on occasions.
◆ are talkative, energetic, daring, curious and impatient; they do not apply themselves well to domestic tasks.
◆ could rebel against strict parental authority and resent strong disciplinary measures.

Capricorn

Capricornian children
◆ may be slow starters but will eventually surpass others with their determination to succeed.
◆ should be taught respect of others as they are not naturally considerate.
◆ have a serious approach to life and seldom use silly behavior.
◆ need encouragement by parents not to worry over small matters.

Aquarius

Aquarian children
◆ are usually popular and make friends easily but are likely to be swayed by the company they keep.
◆ have an equal need for solitude and the company of others.
◆ can pose a problem regarding discipline and may then become ill worrying about having upset people.
◆ sometimes appear to be advanced for their age because of their intellectual and intuitive understanding of life.

Pisces

Piscean children
◆ are sensitive to their environment and can be influenced by bad company.
◆ need encouragement of their talents in acting, dancing, music and performing for others as well as imaginative story-telling.
◆ are often in a secret dream world of their own and can be quite forgetful.
◆ need a pet of their own which will enable them to express their affections and learn responsibility.

Just for the Teacher
• •

Aries

Arian children
◆ require outlets for high speed and nervous energy and need opportunities to express themselves vocally and creatively.
◆ probably dislike doing detailed work and often fail to finish work so enthusiastically begun.
◆ often act impulsively and become agitated and impatient if restricted physically, mentally or emotionally.
◆ have a basically honest and straightforward nature and respond well to reasonable discipline and motivation rather than orders.

Taurus

Taurean children
◆ usually finish set tasks and should be industrious students.
◆ may be slow workers and will require your encouragement.
◆ often imitate what they see and hear and should be guided in their associations.
◆ may lie if questioned under stress and should not be corrected when in a temper.

Gemini

Gemini children

◆ should not be asked to undertake lengthy projects as interest in a topic will be short-lived.
◆ become restless and up-tight if bored.
◆ are good readers in general but are inclined to be too quick and miss the point.
◆ need encouragement to persevere so as to finish what they start.

Cancer

Cancerian children

◆ will reflect the attitudes of those around them and that which is expected of them.
◆ have inquisitive minds and like to know how things work.
◆ may be listless and neglect assignments unless they are taught the importance of responsibility and reliability.
◆ often involve themselves in work or play situations with a great determination when motivated.

Leo

Leo children
◆ love to be given tasks of authority and positions where they lead or explain things to others.
◆ are best disciplined by ignoring their attention-seeking actions for harsh demands may only increase their determination.
◆ need to shine in something and should have their efforts praised.
◆ especially enjoy active games and role-playing, as they can use their acting talents and leadership ability.

Virgo

Virgo children
◆ have neat books and work with accuracy, paying careful attention to detail.
◆ are generally well-mannered and receptive and will expect genuine praise.
◆ are natural students and independent thinkers but should be encouraged to join in group work and be given artistic outlets.
◆ are concerned about their errors and can worry themselves into illness over too much criticism.

Libra

Libran children

◆ respond favorably to praise and need encouragement to complete their endeavors.

◆ can't always explain the reasons for their thoughts and actions as they often respond intuitively.

◆ are best disciplined with reasoning and advice, or otherwise by denying them a pleasurable activity.

◆ should show some artistic or musical talent and be given the opportunity to express this.

Scorpio

Scorpian children

◆ frequently assert their dominating personality and leadership qualities in the classroom or playground.

◆ have a nervous reaction to fault-finding and should be spoken to firmly but kindly.

◆ need to be kept physically active and mentally interested.

◆ have a fascination for the forbidden and may not always follow class and school rules.

Sagittarius

Sagittarian children
- ◆ have the ability to maintain an interest in more than one subject at a time and enjoy gaining knowledge which broadens their viewpoint.
- ◆ will dislike boring routines and won't like a lot of supervision or too many restrictions because of their independent nature.
- ◆ can be restless, active and outspoken as well as disorganized in their habits.
- ◆ are generally bright and alert students with the capacity to persevere when motivated.

Capricorn

Capricornian children
- ◆ are natural leaders and good organizers and enjoy being given responsibility.
- ◆ work hard for their achievements as good results do not come easily to them.
- ◆ can be serious and sometimes unresponsive and may keep to themselves during communication lessons.
- ◆ should respond quickly to discipline but may be resentful of reprimand.

Aquarius

Aquarian children

◆ will not settle easily to routine or detailed work but do have the ability to learn easily if they apply themselves.

◆ need to be taught to organize their thoughts and endeavors or they end up in a dither.

◆ are frequently forgetful, absent-minded, lacking in concentration in class, and may not always follow the rules.

◆ don't show a great interest in ordinary school subjects but do get great pleasure from topics about science, travel, people, exploration, discovery or anything unusual.

Pisces

Piscean children

◆ need encouragement to carry out their tasks to a satisfactory conclusion.

◆ will react favorably to kind, tolerant and sympathetic handling.

◆ love using words and enjoy poetry, plays and stories as well as opportunities to express themselves creatively.

◆ can be abnormally sensitive, obstinate, nervous and easily hurt.

Numerology

• • • • • • • • • • • • • • • • • •

What is Numerology?

Numerology is a study of numbers and an in-depth analysis of the importance they play in your life. Over the centuries, people have made painstaking study of the influence of numbers in the lives of individuals with some startling discoveries.

The number with the greatest influence in your life is the date of your birth. This is known as the Master Number.

What Master Number Are You?

If your birthday falls on the:
1st, 10th, 19th or 28th of any month you are a Number 1.
2nd, 11th, 20th or 29th of any month you are a Number 2.
3rd, 12th, 21st or 30th of any month you are a Number 3.
4th, 13th, 22nd or 31st of any month you are a Number 4.
5th, 14th, or 23rd of any month you are a Number 5.
6th, 15th, or 24th of any month you are a Number 6.
7th, 16th, or 25th of any month you are a Number 7.
8th, 17th, or 26th of any month you are a Number 8.
9th, 18th, or 27th of any month you are a Number 9.

General Facts About Numbers

●●●●●●●●●●●●●●●●●●●●●●●●●●●●●●●●

Number 1

1st, 10th, 19th, 28th
Your
- number 1 represents the feet, chest and circulation.
- jewels are topaz and emerald and should be worn as rings.
- colors are violet, golden brown, yellow and blue.
- compatible numbers are 1, 2, 4, 7 and 9.

Number 2

2nd, 11th, 20th, 29th
Your
- number 2 represents the stomach, circulation and spine.
- jewels are pearls and jade. These should be worn as rings.
- colors are green and cream.
- compatible numbers are 1, 4 and 7.

Number 3

3rd, 12th, 21st, 30th
Your

◆ number 3 represents the nose, throat, heart and circulation.
◆ jewel is the amethyst.
◆ color is violet.
◆ compatible numbers are 6, 9, 5 and 8.

Number 4

4th, 13th, 22nd, 31st
Your

◆ number 4 represents the back, kidneys, legs and circulation.
◆ jewel is the sapphire.
◆ colors are blues and greys.
◆ compatible numbers are 1, 2, 7 and 3.

Number 5

5th, 14th, 23rd
Your
- ◆ number 5 represents head, blood circulation and back.
- ◆ jewel is the diamond.
- ◆ colors are grey, red and white.
- ◆ compatible numbers are 5, 7, 3 and 4.

Number 6

6th, 15th, 24th
Your
- ◆ number 6 represents the lungs, liver and muscular areas.
- ◆ jewel is the emerald
- ◆ colors are deep green, white and pinks.
- ◆ compatible numbers are 3, 9 and 8.

Number 7

7th, 16th, 25th
Your
- number 7 represents the kidneys, spine, gall bladder and circulation.
- jewels are the moonstone and the agate.
- colors are yellow, white and green.
- compatible numbers are 1, 4, 2 and 5.

Number 8

8th, 17th, 26th
Your
- number 8 represents the liver, bile, intestines, back, hips and chest.
- jewels are the dark sapphire and the diamond.
- colors are blue, purple and violet.
- most compatible numbers are 5, 3 and 1.

Number 9

9th, 18th, 27th

Your

◆ number 9 represents the stomach, nose, throat, circulation and nervous system.

◆ jewels are the ruby, bloodstone and the garnet.

◆ colors are crimson, red, purple, blues and green.

◆ compatible numbers are 3, 6, 1, 5 and 4.

Your Fundamental Qualities

●●●●●●●●●●●●●●●●●●●●●●●●●●●●●

Number 1

1st, 10th, 19th, 28th

Shows your

- ◆ mental aggression, individuality and the ability to motivate others.
- ◆ need to take the lead, with the desire to be head of things.
- ◆ need for constant movement and change.
- ◆ ability to absorb information without effort, to remember and repeat when required.

Keywords

- ◆ inventive
- ◆ self-controlled
- ◆ adaptable
- ◆ intuitive

Number 2

2nd, 11th, 20th, 29th

Shows your

◆ tenacity, coupled with your emotional composure.
◆ self-assurance, and the fact that specialization makes you successful.
◆ ability to plot, plan and organize your way of life.
◆ optimism, love of life and your quick awareness of situations, especially when you are suddenly confronted with a problem.

Keywords

◆ sensitive   ◆ creative
◆ original   ◆ diligent

Number 3

3rd, 12th, 21st, 30th

Shows your

◆ mental superiority over others.
◆ high speed and sustained drive and inability to relax.
◆ dislike of restraint and obligation to anyone.
◆ authoritarianism, and inclination to be dictatorial.

Keywords

◆ impatient   ◆ independent
◆ expressive   ◆ positive

Number 4

4th, 13th, 22nd, 31st
Shows your
- loving and sympathetic nature and sensitive emotions.
- attachments to the past and laziness if left alone.
- goals for the future always worry you.
- tendency to play on sympathy and a strong need for companionship.

Keywords
- changeable
- patient
- insecure
- wary

Number 5

5th, 14th, 23rd
Shows your
- leadership qualities and ability to use words effectively.
- tendency to be a good starter but a poor finisher.
- lack of sentiment but regard for tradition.
- inconsistencies in matters of romance.

Keywords
- independent
- impulsive
- volatile
- capable

Number 6

6th, 15th, 24th
Shows your
- ◆ busy and clever hands, magnetic personality and love of home and family.
- ◆ love of beauty and harmony and abhorrence of discord or jealousy.
- ◆ ability to fix any problem quickly without too much effort.
- ◆ determination to succeed.

Keywords
- ◆ dependable
- ◆ domesticated
- ◆ inventive
- ◆ determined

Number 7

7th, 16th, 25th
Shows your
- ◆ desire for constant change and freedom and the need to conquer new frontiers of knowledge.
- ◆ occult powers and clairvoyant tendencies.
- ◆ impatience when you feel things are going too slowly.
- ◆ desire for people to come to you for your services and your need to be around creative people.

Keywords
- ◆ restless
- ◆ mysterious
- ◆ inconsistent
- ◆ idealistic

Number 8

8th, 17th, 26th
Shows your

◆ courage and indifference to danger and the pursuit of thrills.
◆ natural bent is to take the lead, but planning seems to frustrate you.
◆ desire to help others and listen to their problems; your advice is very logical.
◆ need to watch any speculative ventures, such as partnerships, marriage, investments.

Keywords
◆ talkative
◆ magnetic
◆ straightforward
◆ uncertain

Number 9

9th, 18th, 27th
Shows your
- ability to fight for what you want and get it by sheer determination and your strong independent nature.
- career pursuits include writing, publishing, education and teaching. Your artistic pursuits include acting, singing or activities where you can take the lead and be out in front.
- perfectionism, which loses you friends sometimes, but gets you results to the detriment of your psyche.
- need to be understood and loved is your greatest wish.

Keywords
- intense
- critical
- generous
- astute

Your Personality

• •

Number 1

1st, 10th, 19th, 28th
You

◆ accomplish things other people avoid.
◆ have the urge to take the lead.
◆ need time on your own to recuperate your psyche.
◆ are inventive, romantic, sensitive and considerate.

Number 2

2nd, 11th, 20th, 29th
You

◆ are frank, honest and natural in your ways and attitudes.
◆ have a great deal of personal courage.
◆ are cooperative and friendly, versatile and sensitive.
◆ have an emotional nature and should consider partnerships.

Number 3

3rd, 12th, 21st, 30th

You

◆ are alert to change and opportunity.
◆ succeed in your aims and plans because of your tenacity.
◆ have a highly sustained drive but need time off to relax.
◆ are inclined to lay down the law when annoyed and to be dictatorial.

Number 4

4th, 13th, 22nd, 31st

You

◆ are honest though a little bit naive.
◆ tend to be nervous and behave unconventionally.
◆ have ability to restrain, regulate and reason.
◆ are dedicated to your work but can become despondent.

Number 5

5th, 14th, 23rd

You

◆ like to take the lead.
◆ have a down-to-earth approach.
◆ are a very good organizer but avoid partnerships in business.
◆ are a natural actor and always play to the gallery.

Number 6

6th, 15th, 24th

You

◆ generally have more friends than any other number.
◆ have a personal magnetism that can be catching.
◆ are the nervous type, but this tunes up your perception.
◆ possess an impulsive nature, yet you always seem to come out on top.

Number 7

7th, 16th, 25th
You
- give the impression of being restless.
- need to find rewarding goals to operate efficiently.
- are very independent and won't allow people to intrude on your silence.
- have a highly intuitive nature.

Number 8

8th, 17th, 26th
You
- possess a highly magnetic personality and good memory.
- can appear cold but really you have a very loving and understanding personality.
- have a naivety about you that attracts people to you.
- have an attitude of complete relaxation, but underneath you are a raging torrent of nervous impatience.

Number 9

9th, 18th, 27th

You

◆ are an alert person and very observant.

◆ shine when it comes to grooming: "neat", "fastidious" and "perfect" describes you.

◆ are dedicated and can stick to a problem no matter how arduous or tough.

◆ become impatient with others when they can't keep up with your mental drive.

222

Positive Features

• •

Number 1

1st, 10th, 19th, 28th
You
- ◆ are idealistic and strive for perfection, sometimes to the detriment of your progress.
- ◆ are adaptable to people and their situations.
- ◆ are a staunch friend.
- ◆ are well suited to any challenge.

Number 2

2nd, 11th, 20th, 29th
You
- ◆ have stamina and tenacity.
- ◆ possess balance, harmony and artistic qualities.
- ◆ are gentle, adaptive, sensitive, passive and possessive.
- ◆ have an in-built intuition and an ability to get along with others because of this.

Number 3

3rd, 12th, 21st, 30th
You
- have original ideas with an outstanding gift of wisdom.
- are proud and dislike obligations to anyone.
- have disciplines which are strict but fair and you have no grudges.
- love work and strive tirelessly to complete projects.

Number 4

4th, 13th, 22nd, 31st
You
- are energetic but very stable in your efforts.
- are obligated to honesty by your "Karma".
- are resourceful when the need arises.
- are strong and purposeful in your dealings with others.

Number 5

5th, 14th, 23rd

You

- ◆ need to be the center of attention.
- ◆ need to retain your separate identity.
- ◆ have a good sense of humor and can talk and talk and talk.
- ◆ are dynamic and attractive to the opposite sex.

Number 6

6th, 15th, 24th

You

- ◆ are creative and artistic.
- ◆ possess the ability to counsel people easily and positively.
- ◆ are an easy-going type, until crossed by discord or jealousy.
- ◆ possess a youthful enthusiasm which seems to last all your life.

Number 7

7th, 16th, 25th

You

◆ have a high charisma, but need a lot of understanding.

◆ use your occult awareness to guide you and you are rarely wrong.

◆ are inventive, analytical and observant.

◆ like to reduce problems to the very basics because of your emphasis on fundamentals.

Number 8

8th, 17th, 26th

You

◆ will stop everything to help another.

◆ have a simple straightforwardness that makes you stand out from others.

◆ feel that you are different from others; your instincts are strong and positive.

◆ inspire confidence in others and are a good disciplinarian.

Number 9

9th, 18th, 27th

You

◆ are creative and highly productive
   artistically.
◆ love sincerely and faithfully, and
   are always wary.
◆ are psychic and intuitive and use
   these qualities as though you had
   Divine guidance.
◆ like to be your own boss and are a
   fighter for your beliefs.

Negative Qualities

● ●

Number 1

1st, 10th, 19th, 28th
You

◆ are too optimistic at the wrong time.
◆ may lack confidence and become easily discouraged.
◆ are inclined to nourish an inferiority complex and live on your nerves.
◆ don't find it easy to marshall your facts at the right time or in the right sequence.

Number 2

2nd, 11th, 20th, 29th
You

◆ can be melancholic and depressive, causing grief to others.
◆ have a lack of continuity and self-confidence.
◆ become very sensitive if not happy in your associations.
◆ can be bitter, sarcastic and violent if thwarted in your aims.

228

Number 3

3rd, 12th, 21st, 30th
You
◆ can be impatient and demanding of yourself and others.
◆ find romance hard to come by and to hold.
◆ become anxious and depressive over situations around you.
◆ tend to cause intrigue around you because of the way you operate.

Number 4

4th, 13th, 22nd, 31st
You
◆ resist changes and can be too staid.
◆ could find it hard to hold your marriage together.
◆ tend to look at the gloomy side of the picture.
◆ are lonely, naive and need much variety in your life.

Number 5

5th, 14th, 23rd

You

◆ can be easily frustrated and can become despondent or deceitful.
◆ don't finish a lot of the jobs you start.
◆ lack sentiment at times and say unpleasant things to people.
◆ are consistently inconsistent.

Number 6

6th, 15th, 24th

You

◆ are impatient for results.
◆ can be obstinate and at times too demanding.
◆ could be prone to nervous problems.
◆ can find yourself in some unsatisfactory personal situations.

Number 7

7th, 16th, 25th
You
- ◆ are restless and impulsive if restricted.
- ◆ become inconsistent when worried or annoyed with those around you.
- ◆ are a lonely person and may suffer from depression.
- ◆ keep remembering the troubles and trials you have had in the past.

Number 8

8th, 17th, 26th
You
- ◆ denigrate things you cannot understand.
- ◆ are naive in lots of ways.
- ◆ are an unlucky gambler and you should watch this trait.
- ◆ are tactless, blunt and down-to-earth.

Number 9

9th, 18th, 27th
You
- ◆ procrastinate when worried and
  are very possessive of what is yours.
- ◆ worry too much about your health.
- ◆ can only handle one thing at a time
  and have little flexibility.
- ◆ can be quarrelsome or nag when
  you think you are not getting
  through to others.

Abilities of Your Number

• •

Number 1

1st, 10th, 19th, 28th
You
◆ have strong ideas of right and wrong and can be rigid in your beliefs.
◆ have a keen sense of judgment, concentration, wit and the ability to say what you mean.
◆ are a loner, inclined to go your own way; some find it hard to understand how you operate.
◆ cannot hold a grudge even after the most violent argument and you have a strong power of persuasion with others on mental matters.

Number 2

2nd, 11th, 20th, 29th
You
◆ like to see good ideas put to use and adapt readily to new ideas.
◆ have a vibrant and level personality with an ability to project.
◆ you handle partnerships well and guide your partners with your intuitions.
◆ handle positions of authority competently and need work that keeps you on the go all the time.

Number 3

3rd, 12th, 21st, 30th
You

- have a strong sense of duty and obligation to others.
- have a high speed and sustained drive in all your efforts but you need to have a strong personal challenge to succeed.
- have a definite mental superiority, but this changes with your moods.
- can harmonize the most complex problems and situations, and organize their completion.

Number 4

4th, 13th, 22nd, 31st
You

- have a memory that is legendary and a very good sense of recall.
- use your eyes and hands more dexerously than does any other number.
- have more thespian qualities than any other number.
- have a strong sense of duty but not enough when it comes to romance.

Number 5

5th, 14th, 23rd

You

◆ are able to see what is beneath the surface motives of others.
◆ can take the lead in any crisis but are at your best when working independently.
◆ have a good memory and are able to express yourself volubly as required (you do tell a good yarn).
◆ love the drama of power and lap up credit when it is given.

Number 6

6th, 15th, 24th

You

◆ develop excellent relations with others in your peer group and make an excellent leader, supervisor or manager.
◆ do have a need for self-expression, especially in the arts and design.
◆ visualize quickly during discussions and improvise as you go.
◆ have a streak of daring which is stimulated by your intuitions.

Number 7

7th, 16th, 25th
You
- ◆ can mix with anyone because of the power you seem to have over people.
- ◆ possess an originality in your thoughts and decisions and may have a philosophy that seems peculiar to others.
- ◆ are able to concentrate deeply and can quickly sense a problem.
- ◆ seem to worry about the future but your abilities will always keep you ahead of others.

Number 8

8th, 17th, 26th
You
- ◆ need to be allowed full scope to bring out the best in you.
- ◆ have a camera for an eye and a computer for a brain: nothing seems to escape you.
- ◆ are a loyal individual and have a strong sense of fair play.
- ◆ love a challenge and take great delight in winning, especially in sports and outdoor activities.

Number 9

9th, 18th, 27th

You

◆ have a bent for stage work, singing, acting and all artistic expressions.

◆ work at your best when left alone to concentrate and are steady and self-assured, except in love matters.

◆ are reliable and tenacious in your work area and are often copied by others because of your originality.

◆ have a bent towards forward planning, budgeting and buying for value, and detailed work.

Achievements

• •

Number 1

Number 2

1st, 10th, 19th, 28th
You

◆ have a nervous disposition that drives you on.

◆ are dogged and stick with any problem but only after being pushed by your circumstances.

◆ achieve much when alone and you are the type that likes to be suitably recognized.

◆ find it hard to get started because you over-analyze the problem.

2nd, 11th, 20th, 29th
You

◆ achieve your goals by deciding quickly and going after them without fuss.

◆ land on your feet in any crisis and have leadership qualities.

◆ make every job a challenge, the more difficult the better.

◆ have a concentration that can lead you to specialize in matters that will be of the greatest benefit.

Number 3

3rd, 12th, 21st, 30th
You

◆ can create masterpieces in your orbit of endeavor.
◆ play hard at your work and leave others behind in your drive forwards.
◆ achieve progress in the face of all sorts of pressures.
◆ are inventive and clever in design, movement and management.

Number 4

4th, 13th, 22nd, 31st
You

◆ can carry out any task once you have set your mind to it.
◆ can complete any arduous task but need constant reassurance that you have done a good job.
◆ are creative and show a strong artistic talent in whatever you take on.
◆ can make a success out of a mediocre beginning.

Number 5

5th, 14th, 23rd
You

◆ have the push to achieve what you set out to do.
◆ work towards your goal with a sense of urgency.
◆ constantly need to prove yourself.
◆ are in constant turmoil over your work and generally find you are not satisfied with the results.

Number 6

6th, 15th, 24th
You

◆ have a good forward-planning rhythm.
◆ plan to the nth detail and prove successful when unhampered.
◆ are motivated by sensible discussion and good planning.
◆ have an inventive mind and are quick to eliminate the unwanted.

Number 7

7th, 16th, 25th
You

◆ have a dislike of monotony and this keeps you on the move.
◆ respect nature and are able to find rewarding goals in this area.
◆ need to spend time alone to develop your own particular type of creativity.
◆ have an urge to improve your status and are always on the lookout for the elusive opening.

Number 8

8th, 17th, 26th
You

◆ have a number that generally lives to a great age, a longevity not found in other numbers.
◆ like to see your plans to fruition and you have the stamina for this.
◆ have a flair for designing, cutting, making and finishing because of your patience.
◆ have a flair for criticizing and you are generally right.

Number 9

9th, 18th, 27th

You

◆ are very resourceful and a good
organizer but only of other people.

◆ will fight for what you believe in
and have your say no matter what
eventuates.

◆ have a tidy mind and have
schooled yourself to do one thing
at a time.

◆ are tenacious when on the track of
whatever you desire.

Interests

• •

Number 1

1st, 10th, 19th, 28th
You

◆ are attracted to movements, actions and systems that make life easier.

◆ are not physically active in sports and would need to start early in life if you were to have any sort of sporting achievement.

◆ have a good sense of humor; some Number 1s are good comedians.

◆ have a desire to improve your intellectuality and probably enjoy a lot of reading.

Number 2

2nd, 11th, 20th, 29th
You

◆ are inclined to waste your money on things that are of interest, but of no use.

◆ are very fond of children and would make some attempt to have your own around whenever possible.

◆ regard clothes, music, dancing and design, gardening and crafts as coming within your orbit of interest.

◆ have a bent for inventing things and could be very wealthy during the later years of your life.

Number 3

3rd, 12th, 21st, 30th
You

◆ love the theater and all that it stands for.
◆ like to travel and observe how others operate.
◆ are enthused by creativity, progress and stability in others.
◆ have a need to be actively involved in anything in which you become interested.

Number 4

4th, 13th, 22nd, 31st
You

◆ probably have an interest in meditation as you have strong powers of concentration.
◆ are constant in your work endeavors and have a business ability that is unquestionable.
◆ like stimulating interests and have an ability for the theater or stage.
◆ enjoy music and are creative in the arts, sciences and all echelons of industry.

Number 5

5th, 14th, 23rd
You

◆ have an inherent love of travel.
◆ are always completely absorbed in any hobby, but you lose interest quickly.
◆ may take an intense interest in the opposite sex, which could lead to some misunderstanding by others.
◆ almost forget you have a family because you pursue your work with such intensity.

Number 6

6th, 15th, 24th
You

◆ have a need to keep busy and this stimulates your thinking.
◆ tend to be over-possessive of your married children and their families.
◆ have a strong urge to go on searching for knowledge.
◆ feel a kinship with agriculture and nature and probably have a "Green thumb".

Number 7

7th, 16th, 25th
You
◆ need to travel, explore, observe, even if only through books.
◆ have a need to get your teeth into whatever interests you at any one time.
◆ have an intensity in whatever appeals to you but you need to learn to relax.
◆ have an interest in the past and sometimes swing between yesterday and today.

Number 8

8th, 17th, 26th
You
◆ have some affinity with animals of all sorts and you are probably attracted to the country.
◆ are keen on good health and spend a lot of time and money maintaining it.
◆ have a strong home awareness and like your place of living to be in "apple pie" order.
◆ need people around you so as to allow you to talk and talk and talk.

Number 9

9th, 18th, 27th

You

◆ have a great love of your home and your partner.

◆ can be very productive in one field with side interests in others.

◆ are interested in getting value for your dollar, more so than other numbers.

◆ love a challenge and have a good eye for detail.

Attitudes

• •

Number 1

1st, 10th, 19th, 28th

You

◆ are prone to illusions of grandeur and self-delusion.
◆ tend to live in another world, age and time.
◆ do procrastinate at times.
◆ have an ego which tends to bruise easily if you become thwarted.

Number 2

2nd, 11th, 20th, 29th

You

◆ are good-natured but sensitive to situations around you.
◆ make a drama out of everything.
◆ are a natural optimist and can see ahead into the future.
◆ have a good sense of humor and can laugh at yourself.

Number 3

3rd, 12th, 21st, 30th
You

◆ become impatient with others when you sense they have become an obstacle to your progress.

◆ never ask anyone to do what you can't do yourself.

◆ learn to become proficient early in life and people quickly recognize this trait.

◆ are hard to please and satisfy, but you do appreciate endeavor in others.

Number 4

4th, 13th, 22nd, 31st
You

◆ can be sarcastic and cutting in your words, especially when confronting incompetence.

◆ need to be left alone at times to recover your psyche.

◆ have a great need to relax and learn to enjoy life a little more.

◆ show a great strength of purpose when aroused by others.

Number 5

5th, 14th, 23rd
You

◆ have a natural ability for giving attention and care to others less fortunate than you.

◆ become "all things to all people" if this will enable you to reach your objective more quickly.

◆ are loyal to those who have helped you.

◆ live on your nerves and are always looking out for a fast "buck."

Number 6

6th, 15th, 24th
You

◆ are self-contained in your push forward, with a tendency towards selfishness.

◆ have a religious tolerance and that sometimes carries you out of the mainstream.

◆ close up quickly when discord and jealousy raise their heads.

◆ remain loyal to any one cause once you commit yourself.